Marguerite E. Hudson

June 4, 1973

Back
to
Nature
Almanac

JERRY BAKER'S

Back to Nature Almanac

1973 Edition

Nash Publishing, Los Angeles

Library of Congress Catalog Card Number: 77-167515
Standard Book Number: 8402-8056-4

Published simultaneously in the United States and Canada
by Nash Publishing Corporation, 9255 Sunset Boulevard,
Los Angeles, California 90069.

Printed in the United States of America.

Second Printing

To my wife—
  A rose by any other name . . .

Contents

Back
to
Nature
Almanac

Annual
Garden Calendar

This is the first comprehensive garden calendar I have written. It contains brief suggestions for you to follow, insuring your enjoyment of the garden year and keeping you from becoming a slave to your garden. Follow these simple steps each month and you should end up with a near-perfect lawn and garden.

January

1. First, turn your garden over to the birds. Encourage them to spend their time working for you as a bug-catcher and pollen-duster all summer by providing for them now, when it is cold and snowy. Your recently undecorated Christmas tree will provide them with shelter.

Drive a tall stake into the ground and attach the tree securely. Cut one or two branches out of the southeast side of the tree. Leave a four- to five-inch stub near the trunk. Take a ten- to twelve-inch long board, with a one-inch edge nailed on it to hold the seed and lay it on the row of branches in the opening. Hang small pieces of suet in mesh onion sacks in the opening of the tree. Under the tree, scatter bird seed for the field mice, rabbit pellets for the rabbits and a small salt block to discourage these little fellows from chewing the bark off your favorite tree, shrub or rose.

Send for as many of the seed catalogs as you can find. They are some of the best sources of growing information you can use, not to mention their effect on the spring fever symptoms which are now appearing.

2. The pots of tulips, hyacinths, and daffodils buried in the garden in October can now be dug up and brought into a bright room to flower. Bring one or two pots in at a time, ten days apart. This prolongs the spring fragrance and the flowering beauty will brighten the grayest winter day.

3. Sow larkspur and stock seed in large pots and place in a spare room where there is plenty of light. Evening temperatures can be brought down to fifty degrees and days should be around seventy degrees. You will end up with cut flowers in March and April.

4. Melt plenty of snow for feeding and watering house plants through the winter months. Keep your indoor plants out of a draft. Should the leaves turn brown or black move them immediately, they are catching cold. Feed all plants this month with a fish-emulsion plant food.

5. Cut branches of pussy willow and other flowering shrubs and set them in water. They will soon pop into bloom in a warm room.

6. If you need a new lawn mower this is the month to buy one. Prices this month seem to be lower than at any other time of the year. Send your old mowers out this month for sharpening and service, when you'll get more attention and possibly a better rate. Do not wait for the spring rush.

7. Sun scald will generally appear on the south side of young evergreens late in January. Shield them with a burlap screen on the south and west sides. Put panty hose on your tall upright evergreens. Two pair of old nylon panty hose, tied in two bands, should do the trick.

8. Apply garden gypsum to the edges of driveways, roads and sidewalks where thawing materials will be used. This will prevent damage.

9. Make sure bulbs and perennials are covered with marsh hay or leaves to prevent thawing or they will "heave" out of the ground and disappoint you after the long wait.

HOE! HOE! HOE!

It's the home groan of garden work that gives us vegetables and flowers.

GREEN-THUMB ZODIAC

YOU WERE BORN	BIRTH SIGN	BEST FLOWER	BIRTH GEM	BEST COLOR	LUCKY NUMBERS	LUCKY DAY
Jan. 20—Feb. 18	Aquarius	Carnation	Amethyst	Blue	8 and 1	Saturday
Feb. 19—Mar. 20	Pisces	Violet	Aquamarine	Green	8 and 2	Friday
Mar. 21—Apr. 19	Aries	Jonquil	Diamond	Red	7 and 8	Tuesday
Apr. 20—May 20	Taurus	Sweet Pea	Emerald	Yellow	1 and 3	Friday
May 21—June 21	Gemini	Lily of the Valley	Pearl	Gray	3 and 6	Wednesday
June 22—July 22	Cancer	Rose	Ruby	Silver	8 and 3	Monday
July 23—Aug. 22	Leo	Larkspur	Sardonyx	Orange	5 and 1	Sunday
Aug. 23—Sept. 22	Virgo	Gladiolus	Sapphire	Blue	8 and 5	Wednesday
Sept. 23—Oct. 22	Libra	Aster	Opal	Gold	6 and 4	Friday
Oct. 23—Nov. 22	Scorpio	Calendula	Topaz	Red	5 and 4	Tuesday
Nov. 23—Dec. 21	Sagittarius	Chrysanthemum	Turquoise	Purple	9 and 1	Thursday
Dec. 22—Jan. 19	Capricorn	Narcissus	Garnet	Brown	7 and 8	Saturday

February

1. Some evening early this month bring your garden tools into the basement for a cleaning and then spraying with rust-retardant paint. Don't wait until the last minute. If you put it off too long, the dirt won't come off easily. A small, lawn mower sharpening attachment for your electric drill makes it easy to put a sharp edge on your hoes and shovels. Protect the sharp edges and your fingers with "Old Hose Sleeves:" Cut sections of old rubber or plastic garden hose the width of the tool edge. Open the sleeves on one side and fit them snugly over the sharp edge.

2. Check the spreading evergreens to make sure that snow weight has not broken them in the center. I roll up huge snowballs, placing them close to the center of the shrub under the drooping bows for support.

3. If you had crabgrass last season now is the time for action. An early-dormant application of a pre-emergent seed killer on top of a light snow works wonders later. Hope for more snow to cover it further. If you embarrass easily, work on this late at night and it may save you some kidding from neighbors who talk about that "strange fellow up the street who sows something on the snow."

   If you had no crabgrass, and you didn't get your grass seed down in the fall, now is a good time to put dormant seed on top of the snow where it will swell up and be ready to sprout the first sign of forty-five to fifty-degree weather. Make sure the bird feeders are full to keep your feathered friends out of the grass seed.

4. Your garden will wake up with an appetite that would put a pro football team to shame, so why not feed your garden friends early and get it out of the way? Feed flowering trees, shrubs and fruit trees now on top of the snow with any low-nitrogen garden food: 4-12-4, 5-10-5, etc. Spread the fertilizer on top of the snow out at the tips of the farthest branches. Do not waste it by putting it in close to the trunk. Again, work by moonlight if you wish to avoid the eccentric label.

5. Evergreens and your lawn can be dormant fed now with the same food as long as it doesn't have a weed killer.

6. Spread fifty pounds of manure, fifty pounds of peat moss, twenty-five pounds of garden food and twenty-five pounds of gypsum for each hundred square feet of vegetable garden and then just let it set. It makes a great batch of "barnyard tea," which seeps down into the subsoil, enriching it for your early spring plantings.

7. Wash the foliage of shiny-leafed. house plants this month with soap and water. Don't forget behind the elephant's ears. Feed with fish emulsion and poke a child's vitamin or a one-a-day into each pot to supplement the nourishment they miss from summer sunshine. Go ahead, the neighbors aren't watching. Provide a little inside humidity during these dry days by spraying the foliage each day with water applied with an old window spray bottle.

8. Make sure strawberries stay covered with straw and begin your pruning of grapes, apples and all fruit and berry trees. Leave some of the branches on the ground for the small animals to chew on.

9. Grow radishes and lettuce in nine-by-twelve-inch cake tins on your window sill. They'll be ready for your salad in eight to ten weeks indoors. Radishes are planted one-fourth-inch deep

and one-inch apart. Lettuce is scattered on the surface of another cake pan and covered with an eighth-inch of soil. Keep damp and in a well-lit room. Tiny Tim tomatoes can also be grown in clay pots to yield in twelve to fourteen weeks indoors.

SOMETHING TO CONSIDER . . .

You cannot strengthen the weak by weakening the strong.
You cannot help small men by tearing down big men.
You cannot help the poor by destroying the rich.
You cannot lift the wage earner by pulling down the wage payer.
You cannot keep out of trouble by spending more than your income.
You cannot further the brotherhood of man by inciting class hatreds.

You cannot establish security on borrowed money.
You cannot build character and courage by taking away a man's
  initiative and independence.
You cannot help men permanently by doing for them what
  they could and should do for themselves.

—Abraham Lincoln

March

1. Don't jump the gun this month just because we have a few warm days. Johnny-Be-Quick gardeners lose too many plants because they try to rush spring. It's the one season that will not be rushed. Try rushing it and it stalls every time.

2. If you were bashful about dormant feeding your lawn or putting down crabgrass preventive last month get at it early this month. If you are just going to feed your lawn and are not concerned about crabgrass then I suggest that you feed early with a garden food. That's right, feed your grass early in March with a garden food to promote fast, strong, hardy root growth which occurs in March. The top growth doesn't begin until April, so why waste the money? If you insist on raking the lawn in March use only a broom type and remove only what debris will come loose with a gentle sweeping. Too hard and too deep kills the rhizomes. If you did not mow your lawn in the fall and

the tall grass is matted down, cut it on a dry day to one inch. Shampoo turf to destroy fungus and disease bacteria.

3. Dormant spray all of the trees and shrubs this month with lime sulphur and Volck oil. Wash down all of the trees, shrubs and evergreens with a soap and water solution: one ounce of Palmolive green to fifteen gallons of water. This solution is to be used on everything in sight. It works wonders.

4. Don't touch the roses, vegetable garden or flowering shrubs. The only trimming or pruning on fruit or shade trees should be for corrective surgery. Sterilize the wounds with two table-spoons of household ammonia to a gallon of water. Seal the wounds with pruning paint. Sprinkle one cup of parabenzene moth crystals on the soil close to the trunks of trees, bulbs or shrubs that borers are likely to injure. Feed shade trees late this month. Large augers are available for electric drills to dig holes for feeding. However, I prefer the simple root-feeder attachment that hooks to my garden hose.

5. Sow flower seeds in cake pans and flats ten weeks before they are to go outside. As a rule of green thumb, this is the second week in March. Test germination of left-over flower, vegetable and grass seed by sprinkling some from each package on a damp sponge kept wet.

6. Divide and transplant perennials early this month before the new growth gets too long.

7. Don't be in a hurry to plant new roses or trees and shrubs until perhaps the last week of March and, even then, I'm not too keen on it. The soil is usually still too cold for the tender baby roots that have been snuggled up in that warm sawdust packing in the carefully heated garden departments.

8. Plan the additions to your yard and garden this month. Put them on paper first. It is much, much easier to correct a mistake with an eraser than to move a hundred-pound balled tree.

9. Don't neglect your house plants just because you can go

outside a day or two. They can use another meal and shower with soap. Watch for signs of insects. If they appear on the soil, a quarter-teaspoon of 6 percent chlordane ant powder should stop them. For flying insects, spray the foliage with any indoor plant bomb. Begin moving your house plants from the south and west windows around to the east for the coming season.

10. Don't forget your lawn mower is in the shop. Get it out now, before it gets lost in the April/May rush.

A GAELIC BLESSING

May God sleep on your pillow,
May he hold you in the hollow of his hand.
May the roads rise with you,
Fair weather to your heels.
May the wind be ever at your back
And may you be a long time in heaven
Before the devil knows you're gone.

THINGS YOU MAY NOT KNOW

The woodcock's big eyes are situated near the back of the head, and its ears are well forward, almost at the base of its bill.

The opossum is no larger than a honey bee at birth.

The giraffe is as tall as an average adult human being when born.

The anteater has a narrow, sticky tongue that is about a foot long.

Two species of wild swan are native to America, the whistling swan and the trumpeter swan.

Fish are not born with scales. A baby fish is born naked of scales, later sprouting them from under its skin.

April

1. The lawn can now be handled a little more firmly. Wear your golf shoes or baseball spikes when working on the lawn from now on. It helps with aeration. The heavy grass that is now brown and dry is what you forgot to mow last fall. Remember? Next, de-thatch: you can use a lawn groom rake on small yards, a roto rake bar for power mowers or you can rent a power de-thatcher. Next remove all of the debris, fertilize, apply gypsum at fifty pounds per two thousand square feet. Shampoo with soap and water. It's too early to weed and feed, or put down weed killers other than crabgrass control, so save your money and wait for the dandelion heads to "pop" next month. If you want to thicken up your lawn with new seed, make it the second week of April. Any later and you will probably have poor luck. Do not roll your lawn, but if you insist on this process, make it light enough that one of your youngsters can push or pull the roller. There are some new growth inhibitors currently on the market, but my opinion of these is they are still unpredictable.

2. Clean up the evergreen and flower beds and plant annual seeds directly into the soil. Do not put down the garden weed controls yet, as they will destroy the small seeds that you have just planted. However, if you are going to use it in the evergreen and flowering shrub beds, by all means, use it now!

3. Shampoo evergreens and spray with malathion if you were plagued last season. Don't forget to dormant spray before the buds swell up on trees and shrubs. Read all directions before you spray any plant with any chemical. If grubs were a problem, spray the soil with a 44 percent chlordane solution. You can still put down moth crystals for the bores if you hurry.

4. Begin planting hardy perennials early this month, between the April showers. I prefer the three-for-a-dollar size that can be bought in garden centers, dime stores, and supermarkets. Make sure you put the sun-lovers in the sun and the lazy-shaders in the shade.

5. Roses can be planted late in April. Cut new plants back and seal up the entire plant with soil. Leave plants covered until the second week of May when all of your roses can safely be uncovered. Don't touch the old roses yet this month. Just make sure they are still covered up.

6. It's a great time to plant trees and shrubs this month. Make sure you dig a "$5 hole" for a fifty-cent plant, but plant only one inch deeper than it was in its old home. After planting, mulch with wood chips two inches deep. Prune back newly planted trees and shrubs as directed on the package if you want well-shaped plants.

7. It's time for a coffee break for your rhododendrons, azaleas and other acid-loving plants. Sprinkle three cups of used coffee grounds beneath each such bush to build up the acidity in the surrounding soil. And in these days of instant coffees, you'll enjoy the fresh-brewed cups. Do not cultivate under any broad-leafed evergreens as they are shallow rooted and you could cause severe damage. Place three layers of newspaper on the soil surface and then cover with a mulch, wood chips, soft stone, etc. The newspaper replaces plastic for weed control and does a great job!

8. You can prepare the vegetable garden by spading under that mixture of fifty pounds each of manure, peat, garden food,

gypsum, etc., we talked about in February. Do this only when the soil crumbles in your hand. If, when you gently squeeze it, it becomes a sticky mass then don't spade or you will end up with big clots.

9. If you plan on transplanting evergreens and shrubs, early this month is the time. Make sure you take as much soil as possible with each plant to its new home.

10. Feed the flowering shrubs and flowering trees (fruit trees, included) again this month with any good, cheap garden food, not lawn. Do not prune any of the flowering shrubs until they are right in the middle of blooming as they make flowers on last year's wood. To control insects on fruit trees, spray with soap and water again this month. If there are signs of insects add a small amount of home orchard spray to the soap solution.

APOSTOLIC FATE

The North American Almanac of 1855 notes that His contemporaries not only persecuted Jesus but His apostles as well. The Almanac wrote of the fate of the apostles thusly:

St. Matthew suffered martyrdom, or was slain with a sword in a city in Ethiopia.

St. Mark was dragged through the streets of Alexandria, in Egypt, until he expired.

St. Luke was hanged on an olive tree in Greece.

St. John was put into a caldron of boiling oil in Rome, but escaped death. He afterward died a natural death at Ephesus, in Asia Minor.

St. Andrew was bound to a cross, whence he preached to the people until he expired.

St. Thomas was run through with a dirk, at Coromandel, in the East Indies.

St. Jude was shot to death with arrows.

St. Simon was crucified in Persia.

St. Peter was crucified with his head downward, at his own

*request; thinking himself unworthy to die in the same posture
and manner as his blessed Master.*

St. James the Great was beheaded in Jerusalem.

*St. James the Less was thrown from a pinnacle or wing of the
temple, and beaten to death with a fuller's club.*

*St. Philip was hanged up to a pillar, at Hierapolis, a city in
Phrygia.*

*St. Bartholomew was flayed alive, by the command of a
barbarous king.*

May

1. This month we shift into high gear and really get growing.
The lawn should be in good shape by now, turning green with
nice, fat blades. If a dandelion head pops up here and there,
don't panic! May is the time to destroy lawn weeds, when they
are growing their best. Any one of the many weed-and-feed's on
the market will do the trick nicely if you apply it in the
criss-cross method. If weeds are not a problem, feed the lawn
again with any lawn food. Don't forget to wear your spiked
shoes. Aeration is very important to the health and welfare of
your lawn.

If you discover varying size spots and patches in your lawn
check the following: Do you or your neighbors have a dog that

could have caused damage? Dig into the soil and inspect for insects. While digging, if no insects are discovered look for an overabundance of lawn food that may have been the result of a heavy spreader. If your lawn spots don't fall into these symptoms, let's assume that we have an itchy lawn (fungus) and treat it immediately. Poke many holes in the affected area. Spray with a soap and water solution, then follow up with any one of the new turf fungicides, but no mercury. Repeat two more applications seven days apart. Do not feed these areas this month, as nitrogen builds heat and spreads the infection. Mow the lawn at a regulated height for the balance of the summer. I recommend one and three-quarter inches. If you want a perfect lawn then you will cut the lawn when it needs it, which can be twice a week. Make sure that you pick up all of the grass clippings and add them to your compost pile.

2. Trim the flowering shrubs now while they are in full bloom. It is especially important that you cut as many lilacs as possible, if you want the bush to bloom heavily for years to come. These bouquets can improve children's grades (teachers love them) and the plant's health. Begin to trim evergreens when new growth has begun. I usually cut back half of the new growth. After trimming, shampoo the evergreens to control red spider and aphids. If insects are now visible add a small amount of malathion to the soap solution.

3. Roses can be uncovered after the fifteenth of May. When uncovering and cutting back roses, cut back to just above the lowest shoot breaking to the outside. This will cause the rose bush to flare out and keep its center open. Feed the roses with any rose food and sprinkle one-half cup of Epsom salts on the soil around each bush. This will deepen the color, thicken the petals and improve root structure.

4. Don't be in too big a hurry to plant your tender young annual flowers, or those tasty tomatoes and peppers. I prefer to wait until around May 15. Should a frost warning be given, simply spread a single sheet of newspaper over the top of the baby plants and remove next morning.

5. Cut off the tops of tulips so they do not form seed heads. Do not cut foliage down until it is brown and dry. Do the same with daffodils.

A MOTHER'S RECIPE

An unknown writer compiled this recipe, but she must have been a mother:

Light oven, get out bowl, spoons and ingredients. Grease pan, crack nuts. Remove eighteen blocks and seven toy autos from kitchen table.

Measure two cups of flour; remove Johnny's hands from flour, wash flour off Johnny. Measure one more cup of flour to replace flour on floor.

Put flour, baking powder and salt in sifter. Get dustpan and brush up pieces of bowl which Johnny knocked on floor. Get another bowl. Answer door bell.

Return to kitchen. Remove Johnny's hands from bowl. Wash Johnny. Get out egg. Answer phone. Return. Take out greased pan. Remove one-quarter inch salt from pan. Look for Johnny. Get another pan and grease it. Answer telephone.

Return to kitchen and find Johnny; remove his hands from bowl; wash shortening, etc., etc., off him. Take up greased pan and find one-quarter inch layer of nutshells in it. Head for Johnny, who flees knocking bowl off table.

Wash kitchen floor. Wash table. Wash walls. Wash dishes. Call the baker. Lie down.

HOE! HOE! HOE!

The easiest way to enjoy a productive garden is to live next door to one and cultivate your neighbor.

Good gardening is a matter of taking pains—usually in the small of your back and around the knees.

June

1. It's time to give the lawn another light dandruff treatment and a shampoo. You can use the roto rake bar to remove the thatch buildup. Feed the lawn with a fertilizer containing iron. The upcoming hot weather tires the lawn out, so prepare for it by continuing to aerate the lawn area with your spiked shoes. If the weed situation was not taken care of last month you can still have luck in the first two weeks of June. Water the lawn deeply three times a week before two in the afternoon. Remember, if your lawn goes to sleep at night wet, you are just asking for trouble. Have the lawn mower blade sharpened again this month. White edges showing on the tops of the grass blades indicate a dull edge.

2. Feed the evergreens early this month and then cover the soil with newspaper, covering this with woodchips. It will end your weed problems. Water and provide a source of organic food for the plants.

3. Feed your tomatoes with a fish emulsion food. I use this same food for everything in my vegetable garden. Pinch off all the suckers on the tomatoes to improve the size of the fruit. Newspaper mulch in the vegetable garden will save you an awful lot of work and money.

4. Shampoo all of the trees, shrubs, roses and evergreens. Just a pinch of malathion added will get rid of the insects which have

acquired a taste for soap. Six percent chlordane can be dusted on the soil beneath, if any signs of grubs appear.

5. Cut roses from the stem. Do not allow them to "blast" or die on the vine. Remember, when cutting roses, cut just above a five-leaf cluster to promote more roses. Plant garlic or chives between roses and you will eliminate aphids. The soap shower will control black spot.

6. House plants can and should be set out on the east side of the house about the first week of this month. Keep your eyes peeled for problems that might arise, while these tender beauties are exposed to the elements.

7. Large potted perennials are available at this time and can be used to fill in bare spots or add color.

8. Plant gladiolus the first of this month and then again in the middle to insure cut flowers all season.

THE BEST AND WORST OF TIMES

When one is in the business of handing out seasonal advice as I am, he runs into other people who advise by the seasons. My seasonal advice deals with gardens, lawns, flowers, trees, and the things that grow in nature. Others give seasonal financial advice, seasonal health advice, seasonal recreational advice, seasonal emotional and psychological advice, and so forth. You name it, and there's a good and bad season for it.

I thought you'd like to know some of the best and worst times of the year to do a variety of things. For example, research has shown we are likely to be happiest in the summer. The researchers didn't have to tell gardeners this, I feel sure. But women, particularly, are happier in the bright, sunny weather than men. But beware—more suicides occur in the spring than any other season.

Research into technical and educational areas reveals that your brain works best in the spring and fall, the seasons of the most change. Winter out-thinks summer, which must prove that you can't always be happy and smart at the same time. August, it is said, is the worst month of all for thinking (and for a lot of other things, too).

I've discovered the best time to have a baby—from talking to doctors and pregnant ladies, of course—is the summer. This is when infant mortality is lowest, because pneumonia and other children's acute respiratory diseases are at their lowest.

Insurance firms have provided me with a wealth of accident information (fair enough, since I've been providing them for years with a wealth of premiums). June is the most hazardous month of them all. Don't anybody make a crack about June being the month of weddings, either; July and August run June a close second, for accidents, that is.

The worst month for automobile accidents is October. Pedestrians have their most dangerous period in December.

The fall season is appropriately named as that's when most accidental falls occur. Fires in homes are most prevalent in the winter, but are most prevalent in fields in the summer.

Crimes against property occur most often in the winter months but crimes against the person are highest when the temperature is high.

The two months of the year when you are most likely to be bored are February and August. May, supposedly, is the happiest month of the year with December a close second. September and November are generally thought to be the busiest months of the year. People spend more money in December (thanks to Christmas) than any other season, while July is the month the least money is spent.

A commune is one big hippie family.

Education is a know-know.

Stop Air Pollution: Gagnew.

July

1. Make sure that the lawn is kept cut at one and three-quarter to two inches this month. Water when signs of drought appear. It is best not to feed the lawn this month as the hot weather tends to tire the lawn. If you missed any of the crabgrass seeds this spring, they will rear their ugly heads this month. If they are small patches, spray them with any one of the many liquid crabgrass killers available. The soap and water solution should have driven the ants away, but should they persist you can spray the turf area with 44 percent chlordane.

2. It's time to dig up and divide the iris and plant more gladiolus at the beginning, middle and end of the month. Feed the roses and flower beds this month with a dry food—any garden food will do.

3. Make second sowings of carrots, radishes, corn, beets, lettuce and greens by the middle of the month.

4. Trim evergreens, but not too short. Root prune the circumference of flowering shrubs by forcing a spade into the ground the depth of the spade, out at the tip of the farthest branch.

5. Give the roses and evergreens, as well as the shrubs and trees, an early morning bath at least once in July—twice would be even better. While you are at it, shower the annual flowers, especially the zinnias that get so sick in July weather with mildew.

6. Enjoy your vacation.

AMERICAN'S CREED

Written in 1917 by William Tyler Page, clerk of the U.S. House of Representatives, the "American's Creed" was approved by President Woodrow Wilson in 1918.

I believe in the United States of America as a government of the people, by the people, for the people; whose just powers are derived from the consent of the governed; a democracy in a republic; a sovereign nation of many sovereign states; a perfect union, one and inseparable; established upon those principles of freedom, equality, justice and humanity for which American patriots sacrificed their lives and fortunes. I therefore believe it is my duty to my country to love it; to support its Constitution; to obey its laws; to respect its flag; and to defend it against all enemies.

August

1. This is the month the garden year begins. If the past year was an utter flop in the grass department, then here is your chance to build for the new year. We will de-thatch this month. Shampoo, seed and fertilize in that order. Between August 15 and September 30 is the best time to reseed and start a new lawn. This is also an excellent month to sod.

2. Feed all evergreens before August 15 and never after, or you will stimulate new growth which will be wiped out by Jack Frost.

3. Plant radishes, mustard and turnip greens for a late crop.

4. Pinch the mums back for the last time during the first week of August.

5. Feed roses for the last time the final week of August. Give the queen and her court a good shower to curb latent black spot.

6. Wrap up the trunks on young trees this month to save you work later on this fall. This is a must against wind scald and southwest bark split.

7. Apply the parabenzene moth crystals to the soil beneath any plants that borers have bothered, as the borers will be going back into the soil in a few weeks.

BACKPACKING IS BACK

Backpacking is the purists' form of getting back to nature. It's for those rugged people who don't want to come back to civilization—motels and baths and cafeterias—even at night.

But there are some serious questions one must ask himself before he packs it up on his back and takes off. First, do you really like hiking? Not just a mile walk to the shopping center or a friend's house. Do you really want to meet Mother Nature face-to-face? All those strange night noises and weird movements in the dark. Think about that.

If you still feel backpacking is your way out of the grind and crush, then prepare yourself. Remember this, if your feet hurt and you ain't warm, you ain't having fun. No way.

Backpackers have to equip themselves properly, but not necessarily expensively. You have to have shelter, bedding and food. How much of each depends on the length of the trip and the weather conditions. And everything must be lightweight.

The pack can't weigh more than a third the weight of the bearer. It's even better when it's one-fourth the weight. This applies to both men and women. Backpacking, by the way, is a great equalizer—each person carries his or her own load.

You may feel that the extra weight doesn't seem much when you start out fresh or "heft the load" before hitting the road. But that extra weight wears heavier and heavier as the day progresses.

The best distance the beginner should initially try is probably five to seven miles, but only after weeks of walking around your neighborhood to break in your proper walking shoes. Pick a destination that has something to enjoy when you get there. That builds in a goal.

Rucksacks are okay if you're hauling around twenty pounds, because all the weight is on the shoulders with very little padding. A backpack frame helps transfer the weight to the hips, which may be the only time in history where this seems reasonable.

But hips are designed to carry lots of heavy weight, while shoulders are designed to swing through trees. When packing a framed pack, put the lighter gear like bedding and clothes at the bottom, while the heavier food and water should go up high, near the neck, which is the center of the gravity.

When every ounce counts, a down-filled sleeping bag is your best bet, and it rolls down next to nothing. Unless it's the rainy season, a tent is expendable. A ground cover to go under the bedroll and a waterproof tarp will suffice.

A word about waterproofing; water repellency is preferred. Waterproof gear can leak and never dry out. Water-repellent gear, whether bedding or clothing or pack, breathes and permits even damp items inside to dry.

A hat is a must. A tall crowned hat with cut-out holes is coolest. Sun and wind lotion is vital as the food you'll eat. Lots of socks are a must, and most backpackers prefer two pair at a time—lightweight cotton inside, heavy wool outside. Many hikers change socks two or three times a day, drying out the extra pair on the pack frame.

Food should be practical and simple. Dehydrated items save time and effort. Carry a water supply and figure one gallon of water weighs eight and one-half pounds. Wise backpackers carry small, butane stoves for cooking. Wood fires take too long, usually, and I feel it's a good idea to let the used wood stay on the forest floor to rot and continue the natural ecology. But an evening campfire is most enjoyable from time to time.

Kitchen equipment and personal items should be kept at a minimum. A small flashlight, carefully covered with water-repellent material, is a must. A cigarette lighter covered with water-repellent tape is also a handy pack item. A multi-bladed knife is good to have. Plastic bags or bottles are better than canteens, lighter and easier to stow. Always carry water purifying tablets.

All of this is simplified to the utmost degree, of course. With each hike you will adapt and adopt new ways. Professional walkers—people who cover over fifteen miles daily in their work—tell me that the establishment of a rhythm is most important. "Walk easy," they say. Let your entire body walk.

And while you walk, look and absorb the wonderful things in nature that surround you. Spend a few hours researching the terrain and plants along your route, in order that you can recognize the trees, shrubs, flowers and various rock out-croppings.

THINGS YOU MAY NOT KNOW

The word "gopher" comes from the French gaufre *meaning "waffle" or "honeycomb," an allusion to the maze of tunnels the animal makes.*

Unlike the cottontail rabbit, the young of the snowshoe rabbit are born fully furred, with their eyes open, and can run around on the day of birth.

September

1. It's time to give your lawn that final dandruff treatment to get rid of the grass clippings and other debris that you may have missed. If this is left over all winter, it creates a perfect hiding place for lawn diseases to rear their ugly heads next spring. Fertilize the lawn and shampoo. You can still reseed before the end of this month and get a full stand. Cut twice before dormancy sets in.

2. Feed the annuals for the last time to keep them blooming as long as possible. The late food will also be a supplement for next spring. Feed the flowering shrubs with the same low-nitrogen food as the flowers to encourage thicker, fuller, fatter blooms next season.

3. Begin moving house plants closer to the house, onto a porch the first week of September, then back inside before frost comes. Make sure that all house plants have been washed with soap and water before you bring them in to stay. This will destroy hitchhiking insects and sneaky diseases. Place a pinch of 6 percent chlordane ant powder on the soil.

4. Do not let food go to waste in the garden. Give it to your neighbors if you have too much. Carrots, radishes, parsnips, turnips, and other green tops should be removed from the vegetables and left atop the soil to make fresh green manure. Do not grind them up in your garbage disposal; they get into our

sewer system and create nitrogen, stimulating algae. We need the nitrogen in the soil, not lakes and streams.

5. Trim evergreens just so they look presentable but don't go near the flowering shrubs.

6. You can begin to plant spring flowering bulbs the last of this month for next spring beauty. While you are planting bulbs fill a few pots with bulbs and bury them in the ground to bring into the house for winter color.

THOSE AUTUMN LEAVES

'Tis autumn and you have long since grown tired of . . .

. . . *dumping grass clippings so you just let the clippings scatter to the seven winds.*

. . . *pinching off 2,116 dying petunia blossoms so 2,116 new petunia blossoms can take their place.*

. . . *replacing the backdoor screen sixteen times where small hands and yard equipment have punched holes in it.*

. . . *tightening handlebars on three bicycles 123 times, and looking thirty-three hours for the handpump to inflate low bike tires.*

. . . *burning small patches of your lawn with the absolutely positively nonburning lawn fertilizer because you forgot where you'd covered.*

. . . *watching summer reruns on TV and in flower beds you didn't bother to put anything new into.*

. . . *repairing lawn furniture and trying to keep the outdoor grill clean and lit.*

But hasn't summer been grand? I thought so.

Giant Sale: Buy Three Giants and Get One Free.

October

1. Watch for Jack Frost this month, somewhere around the twelfth. Don't let him catch you with your green thumb in your pocket. Feed the lawn with a low-nitrogen lawn food late this month to stimulate root growth, which really takes place after the tops stop growing. Apply an application of garden gypsum to the lawn to discourage complications from snow, lawn diseases, salt and dog damage and tire-track disease caused by hidden driveways.

2. Take cuttings from your geraniums before frost this month. Repot herbs that you want to grow inside. By all means, make sure your house plants are now safely inside.

3. Poke a one-a-day vitamin in the pot of each house plant to help it through the sunless winter. To improve living conditions for your house plants, set each one on a pie tin filled with gravel. Keep the water level at the halfway point in the gravel, but not touching the pot. Set a goldfish bowl complete with fish alongside or among your plants for additional humidity and company. Spray the foliage only twice a day with an old window spray bottle. Water the soil when it is dry to the touch. Later on this winter, watering could be as often as once or twice a week, depending on how dry your home is. Watch for drafts: the ends of the leaves will turn brown or black. If you are not going to use rain water or melted snow it is a good idea to cover

the tops of the pots with a layer of charcoal to filter out the damaging salts.

4. You should get the "last rose of summer" this month, then cover them up for the winter. I use a garden soil-and-leaves mixture, covering up the roses as high as the soil will hold. Thirty inches is my record.

5. Spade the garden, leaving all of the vegetable foliage and green fruit. Just spade it under along with grass clippings and maple leaves. Ripe fruit and vegetables should be removed.

6. Rake all of the leaves off the lawn and use them as mulch in the flower and evergreen beds, under trees and around flowering shrubs.

7. Do not remove the foliage of the annuals. Simply spade it under as green manure.

MAKE IT PAY

Eight hundred-foot rows of cabbage can yield you over one thousand pounds of produce, bringing you about $43 wholesale. Those same eight rows of tomatoes can earn you over $125. Eight rows of onions can bring you in $50. Eight rows of sweet potatoes have a potential worth of $75.

Besides the land, all you need to begin turning your backyard into a profitable hobby are a few simple garden tools, some seed, and time and effort to give your garden the proper care.

Over 60 percent of the cost of fruits and vegetables is in the transportation and handling. That's why your roadside produce stand can offer customers the same things, but at half the price.

You can bring the entire family into this little money-maker. Kids love nothing better than opening up a lemonade stand, but how about this one with real live fruits and vegetables? The U.S. Department of Agriculture has some superb information about growing your own food to eat and to sell. Most of these bulletins are free. Just write the USDA, Washington, D.C.

20250 and request bulletins and a list of other information available.

If your neighbors are of the same mind, suggest a working agreement with them. You'll grow all the tomatoes, while neighbor number two grows the corn. Neighbor number three grows the snap beans and still another grows the potatoes. Each takes from each and there will still be plenty of produce left over to sell or can for winter use. You can create your own miniature farmer's market right there on your block. A series of Victory gardens, but a victory over rising grocery bills this time.

November

1. It's time to bundle up the garden for the onslaught of winter. Lawn should be in ship-shape and all of the jobs done. Don't let your lawn go to sleep with long hair, or it may wake up with an itching scalp. Make sure it is cut to the preferred one and three-quarter inch length.

2. Add some late leaves to the vegetable garden, laying them atop the spaded soil.

3. Cover the bulbs, perennials and biennials with moss hay to better protect them from a surprise thaw in January.

4. Roses should be bundled up now and fast asleep.

5. Early this month when all of the leaves have fallen from the bushes and trees, shampoo the bare wood and dormant spray to destroy over-wintering bugs. This regimen is a must for fruit trees and grapes.

6. Give your house plants a fish dinner every other Friday night to keep them see-worthy.

7. Tie up the tall evergreens with old panty hose to keep them from spreading open during the winter storms and shield all of the evergreens from the south wind with a burlap, cardboard or tar-paper shield.

8. Spray the broad-leafed evergreens with Wilt-Pruf early this month to keep them from being scalded by sun and wind this winter.

GARDEN GIFTS

You don't have to be a do-it-yourself whiz to put together simple Christmas gifts that will delight friends who enjoy container gardening. Here are a few easy hints:

Line an old baking dish with white pebbles, put a few clay-potted foliage plants, in matching saucers, on it and you have a customized indoor garden for window ledge, table top or floor area.

Package gifts of garden tools in clay pots. The smaller sizes, from three inches down to thimble size—just right for growing seedlings—can be filled with Christmas candy and hung from the tree. If you give an assortment of sizes, the pot plant enthusiast will have a complete clay pot "wardrobe" for both indoor and outdoor gardening needs.

Make a long-lasting tropical dish garden with some clay-potted cactus plants "plunged" into one of the large fourteen-inch clay saucers, filled with a layer of pebbles and proper planting soil.

Start children on their own pot plant gardens. A few small clay-potted philodendron plants to care for, and one of the illustrated children's gardening books, might be the beginning of a lifelong hobby.

THE CHRISTMAS GROWING-GIVING SEASON

Here are some interesting ideas and suggestions that should make the Christmas season happy and growing.

Bulbs Hasten Spring: Christmas gifts of professionally started bulbs in porous clay pots that safeguard their health will delight any friend—green thumb expert or not. To attain spectacular flowers in mid-winter, you simply need to add water and colorful buds will make their appearance to herald spring indoors.

Keep Poinsettias Out of Drafts: The best way to insure that your Christmas poinsettias will bloom brightly throughout the holidays is to keep them out of drafts and away from radiators. Kept moderately moist and cool in their clay pots, these sparkling plants will add richly to your enjoyment of the season.

Green Christmas Gifts: Such clay-potted foliage plants as the lush green jade plant, the "Star of Bethlehem" hanging vine, and the Norfolk Island pine are always welcome Christmas additions to anyone's house plant collection.

Pair Poinsettias: An apartment-dwelling family can substitute a pair of clay-potted poinsettias for the traditional tree. Bright, red poinsettias have become the traditional Christmas plant, and they're large enough to group presents around.

Evergreen Ornaments: Small evergreens in red clay pots may be used as table centerpieces, or, decorated with ornaments and lights, as miniature Christmas trees. Grouped, they make an attractive backdrop for a Nativity setting.

Plants Safer in Clay Pots: Make sure that all the holiday plants you give and receive are in clay containers. Clay pots not only have natural porosity to insure proper soil drainage, but their sturdiness prevents annoying accidents of overturned plants during the busy holiday season.

New Poinsettia Colors: Clay-potted white poinsettias make a dramatic centerpiece for holiday table settings. Alone, or in combination with traditional reds or new pinks, white poinsettias are easy-to-care-for symbols of the Christmas season.

Tricks With Clay Saucers: Decorate red clay saucers with glitter and holiday seals and scatter them about the house lavishly, before holiday parties, for use as ashtrays. You'll save wear and tear on furniture and rugs, and they'll add interest, too.

December

1. Pardon the pun, but "this month is for the birds." You might spread a three- to four-foot band of gypsum around all the walks, drives and roadways to prevent salt damage.

2. Decorate the trees and house early this month with

Christmas lights before it gets too cold, and you get in a hurry and break limbs—yours and the plants'.

3. Set out your bird feeders, and the mice and rabbit traps to keep the animals away from your shrubs and trees. Besides they are really great to watch perform through the long winter.

4. Select your Christmas tree early. Make a fresh cut and stand in water in the garage or a protected place. When you bring it into the house, make yet another fresh cut. Gash the bark on the trunk and add the solution of two cups of clear corn syrup, four tablespoons of green-grade iron; four teaspoons of old-fashioned bleach all mixed in a gallon of hot water. This will help to keep the tree fresher and safer while you enjoy it.

5. Have a Merry Christmas and a very Happy and Healthy New Year.

MOTHER NATURE WON'T FOOL YOU

For thousands of years man has been trying to outguess the weather and much folklore has resulted from this guessing game. Strangely enough, much of the lore contains some pretty sound advice.

Even though weather-watching and predicting has become scientific and sophisticated today with satellites and computers giving instant and long-range information, simple signs can still give us the inside on the coming weather. I call it my Big-Toe Weather Forecast.

As you observe Mother Nature a little closer, you'll soon realize she won't fool you. If you pay attention to her weather signs it won't be long until her signs help you plan your days. Here's a year's worth of Mother Nature's signs.

The Fall Signs:

1. When the leaves drop early, Indian summer will be short and the winter will be mild.

2. When the sugar maple buds are fat in the fall, winter will be short.

3. When the leaves fall late, the winter will be hard.

4. When the hornets' nests are fat and low, winter will be cold.

5. When the hawks fly low, there will be much snow.

6. When the pine trees turn their needles to the west, there will be much snow.

7. When the squirrels gather green nuts and do not chatter, it will be a severe winter; chattering squirrels foretell a milder winter.

8. If the crickets sing in the chimney it will be a long winter.

9. When the clouds in the sky look like horse's tails, frost is coming.

10. If the crows do not frighten in the corn field, it will be a hard winter.

11. If the squirrel's tail is extra fluffy, it will be a cold winter.

12. If there is a thunder storm before high noon in September, there will be much snow and rain in the winter.

13. If the worms build mud bumps in the trees, there will be much snow or rain.

14. If the dog's hair is heavy, the winter will be long.

15. If the moss on the north side of the tree dries up in the fall, it will be a mild winter.

16. If the farmer's cat is giddy, the winter will be mild.

17. If the surf roars louder in the fall, there will be much rain.

18. If the hickory husks are thicker, the winter will be wickeder.

19. If the trout in the stream swim in circles, it will be a mild winter.

20. If the dogs sleep in a hard ball by the fireplace in the fall, it will be a long and hard winter.

The Winter Signs:

1. Skinny rabbit tracks in the snow mean thaw is close at hand.

2. Fat rabbit tracks in the snow means thaw is a long way off.

3. If the beaver adds more wood to the northside of his home, winter will continue.

4. If the snow drifts face the north, spring will come early.

5. If the trees split their bark, it will be a dry, warm spring.

6. When the deer reappear, spring is near.

7. When the pine needles sweat, spring is an early bet.

8. When the maple syrup fire's smoke goes straight up, the weather will be mild.

9. If the fire in the smoke house pops, winter will linger.

10. When an old man acts frisky, spring is near.

The Spring Signs:

1. If the land crabs' mud walls are higher and thicker, the summer will be hot and dry.

2. If a thunder storm occurs before seven in the morning in April or May, we will have a wet summer.

3. When the leaves on the trees turn their backs to the west, a storm is just around the corner.

4. Red skies at night, next day a delight.

5. Red sky in the morning is a storm warning.

6. When the birds stop singing, your shutters start swinging, a storm is near.

7. When the bees leave the flower patch, the rains are a'coming.

8. When the hornets fly after sunset, the rainstorm will not come as an upset.

9. When the noon sky turns dark and the wind ceases to whisper, head for the cyclone cellar.

10. When two flies bite, rain is in sight.

11. When the fireflies are heavy, the weather will be bright and sunny for the next three days.

The Summer Signs:

1. If the sun shines while it is raining, it will rain the next day.

2. When the ant hills are small, it will be a dry, hot summer.

3. When birds fly close to the ground, it will soon rain.

4. If the hay field bends to the northeast, the weather will stay hot.

5. If the earthworms leave their homes in the ground, a heavy rain is on the way.

6. If the cows and horses huddle in a field, a storm is on the way.

7. When it rains on the Sabbath, it will rain a little for the next week.

8. If a rooster crows at noon, the rains will come soon.

9. If a cow bellows three times in a row, a storm is not far behind.

HOE! HOE! HOE!

If your garden doesn't seem to be coming along just right, throw in the trowel.

There's no way to have a Green Thumb without having an Aching Back first.

Every man should have his own garden, even if he has to help his wife work it.

Plant a Pencil Now to Produce a Perfect Garden

I am asked many, many questions on gardening every day of the week by people from all walks of life, all over this beautiful nation. But the other day I was asked a question for the first time. A young gentleman from Louisiana wanted the most important ingredient for an attractive yard and garden. I shocked him with my quick answer. "Pride" and "personality" are the two most important ingredients necessary to create anything beautiful—be it a garden, a picture or piece of music. You must first have pride in what you do or it will be done haphazardly. The personality of your creation must reflect the real you or it will appear shallow and false.

For all intents and purposes we're just beginning the growing season. Newcomers to our gardening world—the young couples who have just moved into a new home—as well as the old-timers in the club are just rarin' to get growin'. But it's time to pause. That old phrase, "haste makes waste," should appear engraved on your garden gate and your mind. Plan before you plant is the order of the day. An error on paper can be rectified with a lot less effort than having to dig up and move a ninety-pound evergreen because it was planted in the wrong location.

First off, be button-poppin', suspender-snappin' proud of what you are about to undertake. It will be reflected in the end result. All too often we approach things with a matter-of-fact "I've got to do it" attitude. The end result of this routine approach also looks very ordinary and routine, too.

Design your own personality into your yard. By this, I mean put in all of your favorite colors, shapes, smells and sizes. But first, be sure you only build a floral picture big enough to enjoy, and not so big you will spend all of your time working on it, instead of relaxing with it.

Now a little word of advice. If you look upon each plant, tree, shrub or bush that you wish to bring into your garden as an old and welcome guest and treat them that way, you can't help but have the garden "showplace" in your neighborhood. When you invite guests to spend time with you, I'm sure you make it a point to find out a little about them. Do the same with plants and the best source of information is free: seed catalogs. There are dozens and dozens of different free seed catalog offers in newspapers, magazines and periodicals. Use them for information.

You may discover there are certain plants you like that won't do well or grow in your garden for some reason. You will be doing yourself and the plant a favor by not placing its name on the invitation list. The reasons can be many and varied: not enough light, too much light, poor soil, poor drainage, etc.

Sit down with paper, pencil and ruler and sketch out the border lines of your yard. Place the location of your house, walks and driveways, being most accurate in estimates of space. Now make marks showing where existing trees, shrubs, flower beds and other plants are located. Take this plan with you when you go to the garden center and get the additional opinion of the necessary expert there.

Garden magazines and books are a great place to get ideas, but don't be a copy-cat gardener. You will soon become bored with something that is not your own creation. I have known homeowners, admiring a garden layout they saw in a magazine, go to the expense of having it duplicated with its many terraces, walls, sunken beds and raised walks. It was beautiful, but they soon discovered a problem they had not anticipated: the garden had three fulltime gardeners maintaining it.

You can have a beautiful big home, expensive furniture, fine clothes and a big car, but if you have a poor-looking yard, folks judge by that since it's the first thing they see. You might call your yard your best foot forward and therefore you had better make sure that the shoe shines.

PROFIT FROM MISTAKES

Don't be afraid of mistakes. All men, no matter how big, make mistakes. History teaches us that big men refuse to falter because of their mistakes. Henry Ford forgot to put a reverse gear in his first automobile. Thomas Edison once spent over two million dollars on an invention that proved of little value.

He who makes no mistakes lacks boldness and the spirit of adventure. He is the one who never tries anything new; he is the brake on the wheels of progress.

You will never succeed beyond the mistake to which you are willing to surrender. Remember, a mistake becomes an error only when nothing is done to correct it.

METRIC AMERICA

If and when the metric system of measurement comes into full use in the United States, most of us will be able to adjust and adapt, as the general rule of Green Thumb will still prevail. But just to give you a headstart, here are some key metric conversions you will find helpful:

Mass:
1 kilogram—2.20462 pounds
1 gram—0.0352740 ounce

Area:
1 square kilometer—247.105 acres
1 square meter—1.19599 square yards
1 square millimeter—0.00155 square inch

Length:
1 kilometer—0.621371 mile
1 meter—1.09361 yards
1 millimeter—0.0393701 inch
1 micrometer—39.3701 microinches

Volume:
1 cubic meter—1.30795 cubic yards
1 cubic decimeter—0.0353147 cubic foot
1 cubic centimeter—0.0610237 cubic inch
1 liter—0.2642 gallon (U.S.)

Window Shopping for a Garden

It's that time of year when the seed and nursery catalog houses begin to tease our taste buds with their mouth-watering displays of garden art—plump, juicy tomatoes, rich red berries and crisp lettuce, to mention a few. They then turn right around and aggravate our spring fever with the brightly displayed roses, chrysanthemums and a rainbow array of other annuals.

If we are not careful we end up with a surplus of seeds and plants and a mortgage on the old tool shed to pay for more things than we have room for in our garden. To make sure you get off on the right foot this season I want to caution you early to plan before you plant, be it flowers, trees, shrubs, vegetables or evergreens. To begin, draw your plan on a large grocery bag, split open to give you plenty of surface. Use the children's crayons, marking in the house, garage, existing trees, walks, drives, flower beds, etc. Next, mark off all of your permanent plants, roses and perennials. You are now ready to make additional selections.

Since we must all be economy-conscious these days, let's stretch the green backs with a green thumb. Begin with the things that will feed our family. Let's bring back the Victory gardens and everyone plant a vegetable garden in their yard or a vacant lot that's just lying fallow. To supply a family of six you will need an area ten-by-ten feet in full sun and good drainage, which means no low spots that will hold water. For the beginning or general garden practitioner—one who just wants a garden, but doesn't want to put too much into it—I suggest the following varieties and quantities of seeds:

1 packet long green cucumbers
1 packet Chantenay carrots
1 packet Nantes Coreless carrots
1 packet Detroit Dark Red beets
1 packet Black-seeded Simpson lettuce
1 packet Hollow Crown parsnips
1 packet New Crimson Giant radishes
1 packet White Icicle radishes
1 packet Nabel's Giant thick-leaf spinach
1 packet Rutgers tomatoes
1 packet Golden Cross Bantam Sweet corn
1 packet Little Marvel peas
1 packet Burpee's Stringless green bush bean

1 pound yellow onion sets
1 pound white onion sets

This selection will supply your family with fresh vegetables from early summer until heavy frost. To please the sweet tooth I might suggest you plant a strawberry patch on three sides of your sunny garden. Plant twenty-five strawberry plants of Fairfax (they are the early variety), twenty-five plants of Sure Crop Midseason, and twenty-five plants of Sparkle, the late berry.

If you have a slightly damp spot, but not soggy, then you can plant ten raspberries in a four-foot square between plants. The Sentry red variety is new and tested out to be about the best for the home gardener.

While you are planning your spring garden and still have room, let's think about an orchard. I am not referring to one of those large orchards. I'm just suggesting plums, peaches, cherries, apricots and nectarines. Sounds like a pretty good size orchard doesn't it? Here is the surprise: You can get all these fruit growing on one ten-foot tall tree called a Fruit Cocktail tree. I have seen the trees and tasted the fruit which is delicious.

If you are looking for a privacy fence, but want something more than just foliage, why not train grapes along your fence? They serve two purposes, supplying privacy and food. Here are five varieties you will find suitable: Concord Blue, Niagara White, Caco Red, Fredonia Black, and Interlaken Seedless. Grapes grow in most well-drained soil that has previously produced a garden crop, flowers or vegetables.

While you still have the purple crayon in your hand, let's look to see if you can use a few flowering shrubs that produce a delicious berry and have attractive wood for the winter. I'm talking about blueberries. If you have a damp spot or two, fill them with blueberries. Bluecrop and Berkeley will do nicely and satisfy the muffin and pie crowd.

Pay TV is already here—hire a repairman and see.

Today's horoscope: Keep cool or go to Pisces.

ORBEN'S GARDENING

I didn't do much over the weekend. Just read some science fiction—the new seed catalogs.

I think these seed catalogs are really the triumph of hope over experience. For the last five years, I haven't so much grown flowers as buried seeds.

But each March the seed catalogs come in and you get carried away with ambition, enthusiasm and peat moss!

And they're always cross-pollinating and changing and improving the flowers—as if God needed help.

The big triumph this year is an odorless, thornless rose that lasts for months. I saw one and it's really remarkable. You can't tell it from plastic!

Now comes the summertime. The blood and sweat is over and all you've got left is the tears—when you see the size of the water bill.

Lawns are the passion of suburbanites. I think after that long trip home each night, they don't have energy for anything else!

I've seen stretches of nine-by-twelve lawns that could have been carpeted cheaper!

—Robert Orben, *Current Comedy*

THINGS YOU MAY NOT KNOW

The snapping turtle never feeds out of water because it cannot swallow unless its head is submerged.

Meadowlarks are not larks at all but actually belong to the blackbird family.

A rattlesnake has, on the average, two (not one) rattles for each year of its age.

Giraffes, because of their poorly developed voices, communicate with each other mainly by switching their tails.

Don't Rush into Spring

March, friend or foe to the gardener? It is generally considered foe to the experienced gardeners, because they have learned to recognize March's fickle personality. January and February get most of the blame for March's work. March is the culprit that causes what most of us mistakenly refer to as winter kill. There really is no such thing as winter kill since cold weather and plenty of snow are blessings in disguise. But March winds are another story, and can devastate your garden if you are not prepared.

If March comes in like a lamb with a day or two of abnormally warm weather, we get a touch of spring fever and go rushing out to tidy up the lawn and flower beds to remove the winter buildup of garden litter. This is also the time our troubles begin. Don't ever rush into anything. You've heard that advice all your life. But spring especially can't be rushed. Mr. and Mrs. Green Thumb, you had better believe that if you don't proceed slowly and with caution, March will make fools of us.

The soil in over two-thirds of the United States is still frozen through March. Therefore, most plants remain dormant and are not receiving any nutritional help, nor moisture, from the root system and must rely on what moisture they were able to retain from the snows to get them safely through drying, windy March. These March winds cause young trees, shrubs and roses, as well as evergreens, to actually become dehydrated; thus, we witness the brown needles on evergreens, the black stems on the rose bushes and flowering shrubs. We call it winter kill. It can all be avoided if we will take a few preventative steps, and not rush.

Let's begin by adding more mulch to the rose bushes, heaping it up as high as eighteen or twenty inches. Now sprinkle one-half cup of moth crystals on top of each mulch pile, around the roses. This will destroy most soil insects that stayed for the winter. Spread a cup of rose food around each rose bush, it won't be of any benefit just now, but will work down into the soil and be a welcome treat to the queen of the garden when she awakes. Don't even consider uncovering your roses until at least May 15.

Since you understand that all plants are in the same predicament when it comes to no help from below, we will move next to the shade and fruit trees. If the trees are young or newly planted make sure that you wrap the trunk all the way up to the first main limb. This prevents wind scald which accounts for about 60 percent of young tree fatalities. Spread one cup of moth crystals on the soil beneath to stop borers and other soil insects. Birch tree owners had best make this a must without delay. No need to feed the trees yet as we cannot drill holes in the soil at this time. Be sure damaged limbs are cut off or repaired now before they wake up and bleed to death. Sterilize each wound with two tablespoons of household ammonia per quart of water and seal the cuts and breaks with pruning paint. Regular paint won't do the job because it is not flexible. When it dries out, it cracks, allowing in insects and disease.

Keep your upright evergreens tied up with strips of nylon panty hose until the first April shower, because you never know when March will deliver a surprise late snow storm or hail and sleet. Gently rake the debris from under the evergreens and shrubs with a flexible wire or bamboo rake, then sprinkle moth crystals on the soil beneath, one cup per ten square feet.

Feed the evergreens with a mixture of 50 percent lawn food and 50 percent gypsum. Feed the flowering shrubs with a mix of 50 percent low-nitrogen garden food and 50 percent gypsum.

More flowering shrubs are damaged this month by overzealous gardeners who catch "pruning-shear fever" and cut the blooming life right out of the shrub. Remember this in capital letters: ALL SPRING FLOWERING SHRUBS MAKE THEIR BLOOMS ON LAST YEAR'S WOOD. DO NOT PRUNE THESE BLOOMING BEAU-TIES UNTIL JUST AFTER THEY HAVE BLOOMED.

If it is possible to dormant spray the trees and shrubs this month, by all means do it, but if it means delaying some other job then wait. You will have time the first of April.

Moth crystals under flower shrubs will keep the borers out of lilacs. If you mix one pound of gypsum and a cup of Epsom salt, spreading it around your lilacs, you will have a secret from your neighbors.

Before we start on the lawn, let's leave the trees, shrubs and evergreens clean, wet and happy. Give them a bath with Fels Naptha and water. Shred one bar of old-fashioned Fels Naptha soap into a gallon of warm water and dissolve. This will be known in the future as your "master mix." Pour a cup of the master mix into a hose and sprayer with a fifteen to twenty gallon capacity and wash everything in sight. Make sure you spray inside the plants and underneath—behind the ears and under the arms, if you please.

Two big *don'ts* for the lawn: *don't* roll it and *don't* rake it. In March you only sweep the lawn with a flexible wire or bamboo rake. Do not bear down, just take along what wants to come. Remember what I said about grass seed and crabgrass? If you had crabgrass last season then forget about grass seed until fall, because chances are that any seed you plant will be killed by the pre-emergent seed-killing treatment.

After sweeping the lawn, apply in a criss-cross pattern your crabgrass controller if you had crabgrass, or lawn food if you didn't. Setting the spreader on half the recommendations, spread up and back, then go over the area crosswise. No matter whether you use lawn food or crabgrass controller, apply gyp-sum over the top, fifty pounds per two thousand square feet.

Any steps you take to break up the wind will be appreciated by your evergreens and other plants. I have found that card-board boxes with the tops and bottoms removed make excellent temporary protective covers for young or exposed plants. All you have to do to beat March at his own game is go slowly and surely. *Don't rush!*

POINTS TO PONDER

I kept on looking at the maple tree outside my home in Boston. I moved to that place in October when the tree was in full leaf. I watched it lose its leaves. I watched it covered with snow. The little green flowers came out and it didn't look like a maple tree at all.

Finally the leaves could be recognized as maple leaves and I suddenly realized this had all happened so quietly. The most important things of life are those that happen quietly and slowly. What one sees, as in the case of the tree's flowers and leaves, are results of that which has been happening deep in the ground. It is the same with life.

—Corita Kent

Balance
Your Garden Care

Today's home gardener is bombarded each day with both professional and amateur claims and counterclaims by those in favor of or opposed to the use of chemical controls of insects and agricultural diseases. My daily mail is full of press releases from congressmen and state and national senators, describing the actions they propose to ban this or outlaw that. On the other hand, the opposing team is sending out a steady stream of counterproposals. The result is a perfect stand-off—all talk and no action.

You and I, members of the tax-paying silent majority, must work out our own solutions to pollution. Our actions speak louder than the words of the wheel-spinners. To begin, it is not necessary to choose up sides. You do not have to be an all-organic nor an all-chemical gardener to improve the ecological balance of nature and have an abundant and healthy crop this season.

I favor the "Grandma Putt Method" of gardening. That's when you use what is at hand. Grandma mixed together the organic, biodynamic and chemical methods of insect weed and disease control in such a way that they worked in harmony. She never needlessly used a strong chemical unless it became absolutely necessary and that only after all other methods failed, with the problem threatening other members of her garden.

Grandma Putt had my uncle and me catch toads at the ponds and bring them to the garden each spring. Then we built a small stick pile to house a couple of friendly garter snakes. Lady bugs were brought to the roses and bees were invited to live in the orchard. I was a practicing entomologist—I couldn't even pronounce it—at six years old, thanks to my grandma.

Next, Grandma Putt would mix a little bit of molasses with axle grease and band the trees to trap the insects; place bottle caps of honey near the peonies to discourage the ants from crawling on the beds and spreading diseases, dust the lawn area with bone meal to chase the ants out. On the other hand, she would not hesitate to use Paris-green, lead arsenate and lime sulfur or nicotine sulphate to cure or curb an ill; if it became necessary we intra-planted and over-planted. My grandma was fifty years ahead of her time. It does my heart good when I now see articles such as the one by R. G. Fowler in *Farm Journal*, entitled "To Catch a Lygus Bug—Plant a Trap Crop." In this article he discusses the growing of an expendable plant next to a valuable crop—an expendable plant the insects will like better and stay away from the money crop. J. I. Rodale, editor and publisher of *Organic Gardening and Farming,* is constantly offering natural methods of insect control as does Helen Philbrick and Richard Greggs' book, *Companion Plants and How to Use Them.* Devin-Adair offers sound advice on interplanting. All it takes to have a soft and abundant garden is common sense: know when it is time to turn to the use of a chemical control, use the quantity necessary in the strength that is recommended for the period of time prescribed, and then stop. Practice Grandma Putt's "everyday gardening" and you will be a shining example for the rest of your neighborhood to follow and that's the way to finding the solution to pollution.

NO GAPS IN THE GARDEN

I sometimes feel there is an undercover manufacturer somewhere turning out "gaps," since we seem to confront so many of them today—generation gaps, communication gaps, credibility gaps and so on.

The only gap I like to consider is the one in the flower bed when you have to decide what to fill the gap with when one flower dies out.

I also like to think that the so-called generation and communication gaps do not exist in the wonderful world of gardens. They don't exist because young people and their parents share the good earth, the loveliness of the flowers and the fascination of watching Mother Nature's finest grow.

This is not to say that young people don't have their own ideas of what should be planted where and can argue a pretty good case for it. If parents let the kids participate in the garden and lawn care only as "extra go-get-it tools," then those parents already have a gap—between their ears.

Let's face some facts. Kids spend more time in the yard than you do. Kids use the yard more than you do. It's a pretty inconsiderate parent who would plant a sticky shrub right where third base is, or put a weeping willow at midfield of the football area if there are other equally good spots to plant them.

The younger children can become dedicated gardeners with that special love of growing things if you give them their own special corner or spot to grow anything they'd like. A little prodding from time to time—kids do forget—will keep them interested in caring and cultivating their garden.

I feel that the family that plants together, grows together. Sharing a yard or garden or tree is a special thing. When a baby is born, daddy should go out and plant a tree that very day, if possible. Then the child can watch the tree's growth parallel his own. It's music to the ears to hear a child talk about "my tree." Everyone deserves to have their own tree at least once in a lifetime.

By gardening together, families keep up a running dialogue and that seems to be the big gap-closer. When parents tell me, "I just can't talk to my kids anymore," I simply suggest, "Try listening."

Today's kids, as no others in recent years, are vitally interested in the environment, and the Spaceship Planet Earth, as they call it. You can help them to a first-hand knowledge of ecology by leading them up the garden path.

I once saw a list called, "Ten Commandments for Parents," which stuck in my mind and I feel is worthy of passing on to everyone. These were the things some one hundred thousand children between the ages of eight and fourteen from twenty-four countries listed as the behavior for parents they would most like to see. The Top Ten:

1. Parents should not quarrel in front of the children.

2. Never lie to a child.

3. Always answer a child's questions.

4. Treat all your children with equal affection.

5. There must be mutual tolerance between parents.

6. There should be comradeship between parents and children.

7. Treat your children's friends as welcome visitors.

8. Don't blame or punish your child in the presence of friends.

9. Concentrate on your child's good points and don't over-emphasize his failings.

10. Be constant in your affections and moods.

I think this is a superb list of gap-closing commandments. If you read back over them you see that they aren't bad commandments for the children to follow, too, in relationships with their parents.

Children and young people must eliminate all possible roadblocks in establishing a dialogue with parents. Contemporary jargon and "hip talk" immediately wave a red flag in front of a father who may not be too far removed from "Oh, you kid" or "Cool, man, cool." Young people should work to find topics in common with their parents (which is why I so strongly recommend gardening and anything connected with the outdoors).

Furthermore, children should learn to indulge their parents' love of reliving old experiences even when the retelling is for the fortieth time. Youngsters can acknowledge the parents' point of view from time to time. Young people should also remember their role isn't to convert parents, but just provide insights in why they think and do as they think and do. Parents cry out for clues in this area. Also, young people can make it clear to parents that they wish them to be parents. It's hard enough for young people to be young people, much less parents trying to be young people.

Plant these ideas and thoughts today and watch them take root and blossom. The garden in your heart and mind is worth cultivating, too.

Has anyone asked plants what they think of vegetarians?

Lawn Program

One of the most beautiful sights in the world is a lush green lawn, appreciated by both passer-by and would-be Green Thumber. The man with such a yard is the most envied person on the block, and his advice is sought by everyone. To have such a lawn is not difficult, but it takes a planned program and persistence. I will outline a full lawn program for you, which, if you stick with it, will guarantee your becoming the lawn expert on your block.

In the month of March, broom rake the lawn area with a flexible bamboo or wire rake. Gently, please. Do not bear down and do not use a heavy, steel bow rake. Apply a pre-emergent crabgrass control if you have had this problem.

Always wear golf shoes or baseball spikes when working on the lawn to provide additional aeration (every little bit helps). If crabgrass was not a problem then early March is the time to feed your lawn. Any brand of food will do. However, I highly recommend you change brands with each feeding so that your lawn doesn't get bored with its diet.

Seed in March and April. If crabgrass control is to be applied, check to see that it will not destory your new lawn seed.

De-thatch in April, removing all of the dead and decayed debris and grass. For this purpose you can use a lawn groom rake or a simple lawn-mower attachment.

After de-thatching, mow the dried grass down to an inch so April showers can turn it green quicker.

4-12-4
5-10-5

Spread an application of gypsum in April—fifty pounds per two thousand square feet.

Shampoo the lawn in early April after you have de-thatched, fed, seeded and applied the gypsum. Use this shampoo formula: one ounce of Palmolive green liquid soap to fifteen gallons of water for spraying fifteen hundred square feet of lawn.

If April is a dry month and temperatures are in the fifties, water every other day before 2 p.m. to a depth of three inches. Use a coffee can as a measuring device. Place can in fall of water and when it gets full, that's enough.

Feed again in May with a weed-and-feed when dandelions are in full bloom. Read the directions, taking care not to apply it on a windy day. You can apply liquid weed killer at this time as well.

Begin the season with a sharp blade on your mower and also have a spare blade. Put on a sharp blade at the beginning of each month, and have the other honed. Dull blades smash the grass blades and make the lawn look white.

Begin to mow when the grass is well grown, then keep it cut at a height of one and one-half to two inches all season.

Water as recommended above.

Shampoo once each month to remove surface tension from both the soil surface and the foliage surface. These shampoos kill or discourage disease, bacteria, insects and hold fertilizers in place.

Don't forget your golf shoes—aerate your lawn to good health, both yours and the lawn's.

Gently massage your lawn's scalp in June with a very light de-thatching, then feed with a lawn food containing iron.

Be sure to edge the lawn as overhanging grass will become dry-looking as the heat builds up on your walks and driveways.

The white powder that appears on the grass blades in the shaded areas can only be cured by sunshine, but the shampoo and an extra cutting each week will help.

Green moss in the lawn area is the result of poor drainage. Spike the area and apply extra quantities of gypsum.

July is a month of rest for the lawn. During the hot spell, only water, mow and shampoo. Hold off fertilizing until next month.

Watch for insect and disease problems. The soap should prevent both. Should you have a stubborn bug or two or a lawn blemish here and there, check to see which is which. Bugs are controlled with chlordane, and lawn disease with a lawn and turf fungicide (toadstools as well).

Sow new lawns and over-seed the old from August 15 to September 20 for super results. The later you wait the less chance the baby grass has to get strong before Jack Frost pays us a visit.

Sodding can be done at any time of the garden year.

De-thatch in September about as hard as you did in April, and feed the lawn if you didn't in August. Shampoo thoroughly.

Last of October or first part of November is the last feeding period with a winter green or survival lawn food, low nitrate, high phosphorus and potash.

Gypsum can be applied in September, October or November to prevent salt damage from snow-and-ice melting materials and also to help discourage winter lawn diseases and dog damage.

Just a word here about lawn areas under shade trees. Through long experience, I've found it's a lost cause to expect to have healthy turf under these conditions. I highly recommend you use stone, wood chip mulch or a ground cover in these areas. They enhance the tree, the location and your lawn, as well as save you a great deal of grief and aggravation.

Dog damage can be repaired by spreading half a handful of gypsum on the injured area; scratch it in over the seed, top dress and keep damp.

Remember this: to most people, you look just like your lawn looks.

TVA gives a dam.

Once you've seen one atomic war you've seen 'em all.

THE GARDENER'S PRAYER

Oh Lord, grant that in some way it may rain every day, say from about midnight until three o'clock in the morning . . . gentle and warm so that it can soak in; . . . that there may be plenty of dew and little wind, enough worms, no plant-lice and snails, no mildew, and that once a week thin liquid manure and guano may fall from heaven.

—The Gardener's Year

Beware of
Lawn Blemishes

This section is best summed up as what to do when the "fungus is among us." In lawns, leaf spot and brown patch are the major culprits. Leaf spot disease gives the lawn a yellowish cast "underneath," even though the tops of the grass blades are green. It can be further identified by small purple or brown spots on the blades, surrounded by a darker colored ring. As the disease progresses, the basal part of the bluegrass becomes a sickly yellowish-brown color.

Brown patch usually shows up as a brown discoloration of the base of the grass in times of high humidity and hot temperatures. The patches vary in size from a few inches to several feet in diameter. This disease spreads rapidly and a small patch can grow to a large area of damage in a day or two.

Control of these diseases involves good management and the use of fungicides. Under the management heading, university tests have shown that the use of quick-releasing forms of nitrogen, such as ammonium sulfate, should definitely be avoided. Use the slower-releasing nitrogen generally found in the light-weight "ammoniated"-type lawn foods.

Another sound management step is the method used to water your lawn. Watering at night or in the early evening will produce a layer of humidity over your lawn that plays right into the hands of the fungus organisms, allowing them to multiply rapidly. Confine your watering to the morning or early afternoon hours so the grass can dry off before nightfall, eliminating the humid layer so beneficial to the spread of the disease.

If you must water in the evening, drag the hose over the lawn when you finish. This will at least make all the droplets on the blades run together, form drops, and run down onto the ground.

There are many good fungicides that will work on lawn diseases in the form of wettable powders, which include an antibiotic called "Acti-dione RZ" and other standards like zineb and thiram. A good "mixed" fungicide called "Fore" is now available in garden stores, in both one-pound and four-pound packages. Fore is widely used on golf courses for fungus control, and is considered to be about the most effective.

Fungicides may have to be applied more than once to stop the disease damage. You should mow and pick up the clippings before application. This will remove many of the existing spores and leave the fungicides on the rest of the plant for a week or so, until the next mowing.

Finally, soil-builder type products that have fungicide built into them can also be used. The iron, sulfur, copper and zinc in these compounds tend to help stop the fungus systemically. The added fungicides then tend to knock out the disease spores in the thatch, reducing the danger of re-infestation of the grass blades every time you water.

Liquid iron formulations have also proven helpful in this area although they are not specifically listed as fungicides.

Another lawn disease problem is the buildup of powdery mildew on grass blades. This disease generally shows up on lawn areas close to the house or under trees where the lawn is shaded and damp. Powdery mildew causes the grass to look as if it had been dusted with gray flour. This is the same disease that affects the leaves and stems of roses, zinnias and other ornamentals. Control procedures include mowing, then applying a chemical called "karathane," found by itself or in various combinations. Another mildew cure that can be used is Acti-dione RZ.

Extremely wet weather increases the spread of algae growth in lawns. This small plant is more familiarly found growing in fish tanks, but does sometimes cause a problem in lawns. It forms a thin dark green to black crust over the surface of soils in poorly drained, compacted, or wet areas. To control, use fungicides, soil builders, or liquid irons that show copper in their analyses. Otherwise, read the specific directions on the label of your fungicide container to see if it lists algae control.

Make it a standard procedure to keep children and pets off treated lawns until the sprayed-on material has dried on the grass blades or has been watered in.

Toadstools are another big problem to the homeowner. This fungus is nonparasitic, living on only plant material such as buried pieces of wood and the grass clippings or thatch. Most of them cause no harm. Many, in fact, are beneficial in that they help break down organic matter in your soil. The fungi are present all year, but only become noticeable during periods of high rainfall and high humidity which encourage developments of the fruiting bodies or mushrooms.

There are certain groups of fungi called "fairy rings" which can cause injury to your grass. Actually, the fungus itself does not directly kill the grass, but because it develops a thick, felt-like mat of white mold in the soil it prevents the penetration of air and water to the root system, resulting in the death of the grass.

Early symptoms of fairy ring consist of complete or partial bands of dark green grass, usually in a circular shape which may vary from a few to many feet in diameter. The deep green portion in the band will eventually die and during the following seasons the ring will extend farther outward.

To control fairy ring you should aerate or perforate the turf with a spading fork, spacing holes about four inches apart in the entire area within the ring and an additional eighteen to twenty-four inches beyond the visible limits.

The hose-attached root feeders also are excellent for treatment of fairy ring because they provide holes for entry of air and water into the soil. In this case, holes can be farther apart, depending upon water pressure. After perforating the entire area, prepare a fungicide mixture adding a wetting agent (soap) and apply as a drench. Some suggested fungicides would include Fore and other similar fungicides available on the market. You should apply according to the dilution recommended on the label, using about one teaspoon of liquid detergent for each gallon of water. Preferably you should use a bio-degradable detergent because it will not persist in the soil.

Some gardeners, in fact, have found that treatment with a wetting agent or detergent without the fungicide is sufficient to prevent the dying of the grass. The wetting agent simply allows better water penetration. In severe cases, where the sod has already died, it may be necessary to remove the affected sod and replace with new soil and seed or new sod.

BIG WORDS

Never fear big long words.
Big long words name little things.
All big things have little names
Such as life and death, peace and war
Or dawn, day, night, hope, love, home.
Learn to use little words in a big way.
It is hard to do,
But they say what you mean.
When you don't know what you mean,
Use big words;
That often fools little people.

SEVEN SLOGANS OF FAILURE

"We're not ready for that."
"We've never done it that way before."
"We're doing all right without it."
"We've tried it that way and it didn't work."
"It will cost too much."
"That's not our responsibility."
"It just won't work."

Winter Lawn Feeding and Seeding Produces Prize Winners

I have found over the years that the problem with many gardeners is that they ignore the old saying, "Don't put off until tomorrow what can be done today." All too often we delay chores both inside and out for one reason or other, until a small job becomes a big one or we neglect to do the job at all.

It is now time to start our garden chores for this season, if we want a better-looking lawn than we had last season. The first chore out of the gardening bag is one that I am sure most folks would prefer to put off: dormant feeding. When the snow is still on the grass and the forecasts call for more, that's the best time to both fertilize and sow grass seed.

By shopping now for fertilizer you will find most garden centers and departments have early-bird specials on lawn foods. By doing the job now when you don't have many other jobs demanding your attention, you will have time later to devote to the many other garden areas that will soon need tending.

To begin, if you did not have crabgrass last season then you can purchase any lawn food. Your grass doesn't give two whoops and a holler what you feed it as long as you give it five pounds of nitrogen per thousand square feet a year. Next, follow the directions as recommended by the manufacturer for spreader settings with one suggested variation: If the manufacturer were to suggest you set your spreader on a number six, I suggest you place your spreader on a number three and go back and forth, from east to west and then cover the same area from north to south. Thus, you have criss-crossed the area, leaving no strips and you've covered every inch.

If you had crabgrass last season then you should shop for a pre-emergent crabgrass killer, which will also contain lawn food and selective weed killers. For various types of broad-leaf weeds you set the spreader on half setting and apply in a criss-cross method. The earlier you apply a pre-emergent the better chance you have of killing the crabgrass seed before it has a chance to germinate.

Dormant seeding is probably one of the most effective methods of spring seeding, and will insure germination. The seed is hand sown again in a criss-cross method. Sow it the same time you fertilize, letting it lie in the snow. It will swell up with moisture and at the first sign of warm weather, it will sprout and be on its way by the time the drying winds of early spring come along. It is these early, dry, warm winds that kill new, tender, young grass seed.

When you plan to sow grass seed, you can't use a pre-emergent as it will destroy grass seed as well as crabgrass seed.

You are probably wondering what your neighbors will think when they look out of their window and see you all bundled up in your mackinaw, ear muffs and scarf pushing your lawn spreader through the snow. Probably the same thing my neighbors thought of me the first time they saw me doing this same job. "Ol' Baker has flipped his lid," they said. But they changed their tune. They were the first ones out the next winter.

Golf courses and yards have been spreading fertilizer for the last month and a half. When it comes to growing things properly professionals never stand on the phrase, "for appearance sake." Results are all the pros are interested in.

It is best to do your dormant feeding, weeding and seeding on a day when the snow is down enough, so it won't touch the holes in your spreader, clogging it up.

While you are all bundled up for the weather there is one more job for you and your spreader. This is a professional secret. If you or the city have used salt for melting snow and ice, there is a distinct possibility of salt damage to the turf area next to walks, patios, drives and roadways. This damage can be corrected or prevented by making an application of gypsum three feet wide along the edges of these iced areas.

If heavy clay soil is your problem then you will spread fifty pounds of gypsum per thousand square feet, on top of the snow, on the lawn and in the evergreen buds to break up this heavy soil.

I am a firm believer that "seeing is believing." If you want to see the greenest, thickest, healthiest lawn you have ever had, believe me, bundle up and dormant feed your garden today without delay.

EXCUSES, EXCUSES, EXCUSES

One of the pleasures of getting around this great country and alking to people about their gardens and ecology programs and growing things is finding out most people procrastinate like I do n many areas.

I gather a whole new batch of excuses to use as I travel about nd hear people offer lame excuses why they can't have a great yard, garden and landscape. Here are some real excuses you, too, can use:

"Our kids fed all the seed to the birds."
"Our neighbors never returned the garden tools they borrowed."
"My blisters from last year didn't heal."
"All the kids in the neighborhood think our yard is a playground and walk-through."
"When I bend down to plant, my kids jump on my back."
"The sun never shines on this part of our yard."
"We got the rockiest lot in the subdivision, and what's not rock, is sand and clay."
"Our neighbors let their dogs run free at night."
"I really think I may concrete it over and paint it green."
"I reallly think I may put in Astroturf."
"I really think I may move."

GUN CARE

A bit too much grease in the barrel or chamber of a high-powered, center-fire rifle is an invitation to trouble.

It causes an extreme buildup of pressure when the shell explodes. Too much oil can also result in excessive pressures and could burst the weapon.

Sportsmen who allow snow or mud or some other obstruction in the muzzle are also asking for trouble. Shotguns have been known to peel back like a banana when an obstruction prevents the pressure from going out with the shot.

In extreme cold, too much oil also slows down action, collects dirt and freezes in winter. It could also soften and weaken the stock.

When the shell explodes in the chamber, back pressure could also cause oil to squirt in your eye!

—Jerry Chiappetta

Solve
Your Soggy Spot and
Drainage Problems

In every gardener's life a soggy spot or two will arise, causing many moments of anguish. But worry no longer, my gardening friends, for you can end this problem without another hour of worry.

To begin, you must understand the reasons for excessive moisture and recognize them immediately. The most common, most aggravating is moss growing where you had hoped you would have grass. Moss will grow and thrive where good grasses wouldn't have a chance, thus adding fuel to the old stories that moss is a sign of acid or sour soil. This may be the cause in some cases, but very few. Most green moss problems are caused by one or more of these four basic growing conditions. Check to see if any of them exist around your problem spot.

First is lack of sufficient food (fertilizer), probably the prime reason why moss grows and thrives under most large, shade trees. We fail to apply enough food for the needs of the trees, shrubs and grasses. To eliminate this condition, feed the trees and shrubs with a root feeder, forcing the food down below the turf-root area where the tree will benefit. Apply a good balanced lawn food to the grass area beneath, twice as often as you do the rest of the lawn. If you have flowering shrubs such as azaleas beneath a tree, a surface feeding of 5-20-20 or 6-10-4 will keep them happy and your green moss problem should go away because the soil will be too rich for it to survive.

The next most common problem is shade. There are very few of the good grasses that will grow in any kind of a shaded area, even the fescues that are recommended won't do well in a heavily-shaded area. When the grass vacates, the moss moves in. To improve the shady situation, one can do some thinning of branches if a tree is the shading object. This trimming will in most cases help the tree as well as the soil below. Along with the thinning, add liberal quantities of common rye grass (inexpensive) every three weeks which will germinate in twelve to eighteen days, thus giving you a constant supply of new grass.

Another cause of green moss is constant soil moisture. Water collecting on the soil surface creates the type of soil condition moss really loves. To reduce this problem to a manageable level, poke holes in the area with the help of a hammer and steel pole, pipe, wooden stake or a tree auger, which will fit most electric drills. Bore the holes eighteen to twenty-four inches deep or deeper and fill with sharp sand or gravel, mixed half-and-half with gypsum. You can also apply gypsum over the soggy area and half the distance beyond (twenty-five pounds per five hundred square feet). If the area is a very large one it may be advisable to lay drain tiles below the ground. A visit to your local farm supply and equipment store can provide you with the necessary information for this project.

Now the remaining cause is the combination of all of these problems, allowed to continue for too long a period of time, resulting in a highly acid soil condition. This is often called "sour soil." Some lawn experts would advise you that an application of lime will correct or remedy this problem, but rarely will this help. You must correct each of the causes. There is, of course, a bright side to the acid soil condition which can be used to an imaginative gardener's benefit. Plant broad-leafed flowering shrubs beneath large shade trees where they will thrive with a little care and cause no problems.

Now let's move out into the open with our soggy situation. Oh yes, you don't need the shade from trees alone to cause an excess moisture soil situation. All we need is a builder who hauled in expressway clay to build our lots, and we will end up with a soggy situation that drowns out our gardening endeavor. This problem can be whipped, resulting in a very pleasant and most attractive landscape design. I call the method "used surface" planting. Have good, rich, sandy loam hauled in and deposited in contour piles in various locations on your property—any place you want to plant a tree, shrub, evergreen or flower bed. These piles of soil will run as high as three feet, if you are planning on planting a large birch or maple clump, down to six inches for a flower bed.

To sculpture the soil surface, add large quantities of gypsum (fifty pounds per five hundred square feet) tilled into the clay area beyond. Now lay your sod on the sides of the soil mounds leaving the planting areas open at the tops. Plant any trees you have selected in the mounds, mulch with wood chips and watch your garden grow. Have no fear of excess water destroying your previous and expensive plants, because the water will run down through the pile and out along the clay surface below to the waiting sod roots.

To see examples of used surface planting, just visit new home models and note how the landscape designers use this almost exclusively on land developments making excessive use of clay.

HOE! HOE! HOE!

If you wish to bridge the vegetable food costs, try leading with a spade.

Never plant more lawn and yard than your spouse can take care of.

Love thy neighbor if he has yard tools you'd rather borrow than buy.

Optimistic gardeners believe what goes down must come up.

Whoever draws pictures on seed catalogs, also writes the "rave" reviews of shows in the TV listings.

NOTICE

The objective of all dedicated gardeners should be to thoroughly analyze all situations, anticipate all problems prior to their occurrence, have answers for these problems, and move swiftly to solve these problems when called upon.

However, when you are up to your ass in alligators, it is difficult to remind yourself that your initial objective was to drain the swamp.

Community Gardening

When a newsman interviews a professional athlete, artist or expert in any given field, you can be sure this question will be asked: "When did you first become interested in your field?" The answer, more often than not, is "When I was just a small child."

It is a fact that if you introduce a talented child to a particular activity when he is young, then encourage and counsel the youngster on proper performance and technique, there is an excellent chance that he will turn into a real pro. This works in athletics, the arts, such domestic subjects as cooking and sewing, as well as the sciences. Works, that is, if the child also has a natural talent for the subject.

Parents transport children halfway across the city for a hockey, music or art lesson. Parents forego their own plans to supervise cookie, candy or bake sales to raise funds to finance the worthwhile projects which shape the futures of their children.

But as responsible modern adults we neglect an important phase in the education of today's youth, a phase that was an important, popular factor in our own youth. The phase of our neglect is that of the earth sciences—gardening! I remember in the early 1940s, every spring we would bring home order forms from school, listing all of the many vegetables and flower seeds that were available for planting a Victory garden. Our parents would make their selections and we would return the list and our pennies to the school. When the seed arrived, most of us ran all the way home with the packets and badgered our folks to get started on the garden. Some families were fortunate enough to have a garden spot close to home, while others had to walk or drive several miles to the city, state or county land that was designated for Victory gardens. We all helped and enjoyed growing together. We were practicing back-to-earth ecology, as a matter of fact, from about 1934 to 1947. The American public did more in the fields of conservation and ecology then than any other time in our modern history. It's a historical fact that hard and sad times are the reasons for a return to nature, as in the aftermath of a Depression and during World War Two. These traumatic and frustrating times are both hard and sad. So let's return to the days of yesteryear when a packet of seed could excite the whole family. Not many things are capable of doing that today.

This is the way we can make professional gardeners out of the next generation and polish up our own Green Thumb at the same time. Science teachers can begin by teaching basic fundamentals of enriching the soil by composting, which helps grow healthy fruits and vegetables, schools can make arrangements with local merchants to supply garden seeds for sale through school projects. Land developers, holding large parcels of till-able land on speculation, could have it plowed and disked, then rented out in plots to local families for the cost of the plowing and disking. Communities could hold contests, awarding prizes by age groups. An overabundance of fresh produce could also help feed the needy.

Local garden clubs can supply information. Landscapers along with parks and recreation departments can supply compost and wood chips.

There are so many advantages to this type of project: fallow land is enriched, eyesores are removed, development of community cooperation, early ecology education of our youth, fresh produce for the table, etc.

Everybody has something to say about the pollution problem and our neglect of the earth. Here is your chance to do something: "Put your muscle where your mouth is." Communities that sow together will grow together.

The Compatible Vegetable Garden

Symbiosis, a word unfamiliar to most gardeners, holds the secret to a successful, abundant vegetable garden.

Symbiosis, as described by Webster, means "the intimate living together of two dissimilar organisms in a mutually beneficial relationship." To simplify this description even more and associate it directly with our gardens, it means the growing together of two different type plants, one to the benefit of the other. If man would practice "human symbiosis" in his everyday living, this world might just turn out to be a Garden of Eden.

I refer to this method as "brotherhood gardening," and attempt to interplant vegetables and flowers together. This has a dual purpose, either protecting one another from insects and disease, or adding to or extracting from the soil some beneficial ingredient the other can use.

We have for too many years planted the traditional vegetable or flower gardens. All flowers or all vegetables, and in a stereotyped fashion: a row of radishes, corn, carrots, and lettuce, making sure each was kept separated from the other and in a straight line. We also plant the same thing in the same spot, year in and year out, then wonder why each year the production gets less and less. Each plant extracts certain elements from the soil to stabilize its system. After a couple of years in the same spot, the plant tends to take all of that element from the surrounding soil. We have to assume the Indians were right when they taught our forefathers to rotate crops each year.

Next we must fortify the flower and vegetable garden each year by mixing up a batch of Barnyard Tea. This is done with fifty pounds of manure, fifty pounds of peat moss, twenty-five to fifty pounds of garden gypsum and twenty-five pounds of garden food. Spread this, along with liberal quantities of leaves, over each hundred to hundred and fifty square feet of garden area in the fall, winter or the very early spring.

Barnyard Tea should be spaded into the soil in early May, when the soil will crumble in your hand. This procedure returns more of the elements that your plants have extracted.

Next, we get down to the basis of symbiosis: the selection of proper neighbors. From the outset, you must understand that we *do not* keep flowers, vegetables and fruits apart. We are going to mix them up whenever and wherever they will benefit each other. The old habit we developed of straight-line planting is another habit we must break. Contour planting can prevent excessive water run-off, which carries away valuable soil (through erosion) and causes precious loss of food and other trace elements. Last but not least, you can have a very attractive and unusual garden. Let's take a look at the plants that will best benefit each other in one way or another.

PLANT VARIETY	GOOD NEIGHBOR
asparagus	tomato, parsley
bean	corn, carrot, cauliflower, beet, cucumber, cabbage, potato, celery
beet	onion, bean, kohlrabi
broccoli, cabbage	dill, potato, sage, rosemary, mint
carrot	lettuce, chives, onion
cauliflower	(see cabbage)
celery	bean
corn	potato, bean, pea, melon, squash, pumpkin, cucumber
cucumber	corn, potato, cabbage, radish
lettuce	strawberry, carrot, radish
onion	beet, carrot
pea	radish, carrot, cucumber corn bean, turnip, pea
potato	bean, sweet corn, cabbage pea, marigold, bean, horse-radish
pumpkin	corn
radish	pea, lettuce, nasturtium, cucumber
spinach	strawberry
tomato	cabbage, parsley, marigold, potato, cucumber
fruit tree	chives, nasturtium, garlic
grape	mustard green
strawberry	bean, lettuce and spinach
rose	garlic, onion, chives, marigold

This only suggests where you might start. Your own experiments will lead you into exciting pathways of home gardening.

THINGS YOU MAY NOT KNOW

The eggs of snapping turtles are good food but must be fried as they will not boil hard.

A dragonfly can use its feet for perching on a limb but its legs are useless for walking.

PLANT A GARDEN

If your purse no longer bulges and you've lost your golden treasure,
If at times you think you're lonely and have hungry grown for pleasure,
Don't sit by your hearth and grumble—don't let mind and spirit harden.
If it's thrills of joy you wish for, get to work and plant a garden.
If it's drama that you sigh for, plant a garden and you'll get it.
You will know the thrill of battle fighting foes that will beset it.
If you long for entertainment and for pageantry most glowing,
Plant a garden, and this summer spend your time with green things growing.
If it's comradeship you sigh for, learn the fellowship of daisies.
You will come to know your neighbor by the blossoms that he raises;
If you'd get away from boredom and find new delights to look for,
Learn the joy of budding pansies which you've kept a special nook for.

If you ever think of dying, and you fear to wake tomorrow,
Plant a garden! It will cure you of your melancholic sorrow.
Once you've learned to know the peonies, petunias and roses,
You will find that every morning some new happiness discloses.

—Edgar A. Guest

Vegetable Garden Summer Care

It's time to turn our attention to the vegetable garden to insure that we get our share of the harvest. We are not the only ones waiting for the radishes to ripen. Wooly Worm and Creepy Crawler are patiently waiting, too. But there are more important things to do than be bugged about bugs, if we are going to end up with a bumper crop. Let's get growing.

Tomatoes are our initial concern, as they are America's most popular home garden crop. Corn, by the way, is second. Let's get the pest problem out of the way first. If you are applying a shampoo from time to time, you shouldn't have anything to buy. But if the Tomato Horne Bore—that big, fat, green worm—shows up, use a broad-spectrum insecticide. It will handle any insect that is bumming in your garden. You can continue to plant tomatoes into July and be assured of a late harvest.

When planting tomatoes be sure to plant them deep enough so that the bottom row of leaves are flush with the ground, which assures a longer rooting area.

Tomatoes, cucumbers, squash and the vine crops can't compete with weeds. So it is a must to keep them happy and weed-free. There are several simple and time-saving ways, one is the application of the chemical garden weeders that are now available. Another method is to plant through holes in sheets of black plastic or plastic cleaning bags. You also can use newspapers as a mulch or grass clipping, wood chips, etc. Any one of these will control the weeds. Personally, I prefer the newspaper as I can then spade it into the soil for next season, helping to condition the soil. Try different methods to see which you like best.

Feed your tomatoes on a regular basis. I use the "little bit, lots of times" method, as opposed to "lots of food, one time." Use a 5-20-20 dry and any of the fish emulsions whenever you get the ambition. The same goes for the rest of the vegetable garden.

Keep your eyes open for sick plants. Blossom-end rot will most likely be the big problem. This is when the blossom end of the tomatoes turns gray, then black. This problem is caused by poor distribution of moisture in hot, dry weather. It can be controlled by spraying with a solution of one tablespoon of calcium chloride to a gallon of water. If you want to narrow down the rot possibility, plant Marglobe tomatoes.

To avoid sick tomatoes be sure to wash your hands well before you work in the garden, particularly if you are a smoker as tomatoes are susceptible to diseases transported through tobacco smoke. If you have been bothered in the past with diseases, try a spray made with one part skimmed milk to nine parts of water.

The real idea of the tomato game is to get all of the tomatoes you can to grow on each vine. For this we need lots of blossoms to stick and form fruit. You can do this by spraying the flowers with any one of the tomato-set sprays, which comes in an aerosol can. Spray any of your melon and other vine flowers to insure a higher yield.

It is an excellent idea to stake your tomatoes and train them to grow up off the ground. This makes caring for them easier, as well as discouraging disease and insect problems. The method or style can be with a single pole, tying the plant as it grows with small strips of panty hose or make a three-stick tepee over the vine top and wind it around. Other vine crops should be kept up as well, and this can be accomplished by placing small twigs beneath the plants as they grow out. Try it, and you'll soon see the difference. While I am on the ADP (Aid to Dependent Plants) subject, bush beans will yield more if a light branch is placed beneath. Pole beans can be trained to climb a wire or wooden fence and it looks great, too.

Don't water your tomatoes from the top. Water from below, and water deep.

Now then, let's get to the key step in tomato care and culture: pruning and suckering. Tomato plants can be pruned by pinching the tops out in the late summer. This keeps them short and bushy.

After they have formed all the fruit, the additional "extra" growth food that could be going to other areas of the plant is being taken by the suckers: these are free-loading rascals that are just along for the ride. They eat a lot and don't work. Suckers hide, but here is how you find them. Put your left hand out in front of your face, next extend your thumb out and down as far as it will go. In the pocket of the V your index finger and thumb make is where the sucker on your tomato hides; he grows out between the main stalk and the foliage stem. Pinch him off whenever you see him.

That's it for tomatoes. Let's take a quick look at the other vegetables. Check the beets, carrots, parsnips and other below-the-ground crops for maggots if they are around. Then spray the soil with 44 percent chlordane. You can also feed the vegetable garden with 5-20-20 now as a boost.

Look over the peppers, potatoes and squash for the Tomato Horne Bore (oh, yes, he likes these vegetables better than tomatoes) and spray with a broad-spectrum insecticide.

If you are mulching with newspaper, you won't have a weed problem so relax and enjoy.

Where there's smoke there's fuzz.

WHY DON'T THEY . . .

Sometimes a little garden day-dreaming is fun. I often wonder why don't they . . .

. . . develop a tomato that separates into sections like an orange by merely pulling it apart?

. . . create a yard in squares you can replace like the worn-out pieces of tile on a floor?

. . . breed a strain of patio shrub or flower that would give off a fragrance which would do one of two things: lure mosquitoes and pesky insects to it where they would get stuck; or would set up a barrier that would throw them off?

. . . develop a potato that grows in sections ready to French fry, or slit ready for cheese stuffing?

. . . come out with an onion that grows in a chopped and diced state?

. . . figure out a way for a Jack O' Lantern pumpkin to grow pre-hollowed?

According to the Agricultural Research Service, there is a possibility plant physiologists will actually develop a blue rose in the near future.

According to the U.S. National Arboretum researcher, Dr. Don Egolf, the Rose-of-Sharon tree is being made more suitable for urban planting. These researchers have created a mildew-resistant *Pyracantha*, and double-flower crab apple apples.

Maybe a sectioned tomato is not so farfetched, but I have doubts that a pre-crinkle-cut potato will make it.

HOE! HOE! HOE!

One of gardening's biggest problems—sustaining April's enthusiasm when sweltering July is at hand.

78   *Back to Nature Almanac*

CUSTOMS' CUSTOMS

If your getting back to nature is going to take you through customs, may I offer you this piece of advice: customs officials suspect everyone. They particularly suspect those who worry about being suspected.

Customs of the customs inspectors can help, though. For example, fat people are automatically suspect, because customs has seen too many phony bellies and padded thighs.

Customs officials tend to pass through families, particularly large ones with crying babies, faster than most anyone else.

Don't steal hotel ashtrays or towels. When an inspector finds loot like that, he automatically suspects what sort of person you are and will give everything you bring in a going-over.

If you do stash your contraband away, hide it in a nice place. Customs inspectors have a dislike for rummaging through dirty clothes and dirty baby diapers. Finding no-no's there will make them slap you with the stiffest penalties.

Many people believe that if you pass through customs at a busy time of the day or night, you'll get by easier. Long lines of cars can make inspectors rush, but those horn-honkers can also make the inspectors irritable and touchy.

Don't kid around with the customs officials as they've heard all the jokes, quips and one-liners. If you have a choice, pick a younger inspector who doesn't have the "ring savvy" of the older customs man. But the younger man may be eager to prove he's a super sleuth.

One last bit of advice: read up on what you can and can't bring in and use this knowledge accordingly.

THINGS YOU MAY NOT KNOW

The trumpeter swan, with a maximum weight of forty pounds, is the heaviest flying bird in North America.

Like the chameleon, the tree toad can change its color to blend with tree bark or the bright green of new leaves.

Supercharge Your Gardening

I am sure that if a survey was taken on the most discussed subject in the summertime, weather would win hands down. City fellers and country folks are all concerned with the immediate weather forecast for varying reasons. The city and country farmers would give a big red apple if they could control the weather for the benefit of their gardens and crops.

To some extent you can control the benefits of the weather, or at least create the same effects which certain weather conditions contribute. There is an extremely fertile effect a thunder-and-lightning storm has on your garden and lawn. Immediately after one of these supercharged storms your plants seem to literally turn green instantly. Fact of the matter, my friends, is they do, as a result of the electrically charged oxygen which is turned into 78 percent nitrogen.

You can create this same condition in your garden simply by practicing a special type of gardening called *electroculture.* Electroculture is gardening with the use of metal objects, such as copper wire, metal trellises and tin cans which will attract the static electricity in the vicinity of your vegetable garden. This charges the atmosphere, giving you additional help from Mother Nature in the form of pure, gentle and free-growing elements which will increase the size, health and yield of your garden.

First, stretch a piece of fine copper wire over the top of your vegetables, and fasten it to wooden stakes at each end of the row. Place wire high enough so that it does not touch tree plants.

Another method is to place tin cans every twelve to eighteen inches apart in your row with the tops and bottoms removed. Bury the first two inches of the can in the ground to keep it from falling over.

Melon and other vine crops, including beans, can be grown on metal fences, resulting in some of the most fascinating and extraordinary results.

Whenever possible, use copper, which gives better results. For more information on the use of copper in gardening and farming you might write to Phelps Dodge Industries, 300 Park Avenue, New York, N. Y. Phelps Dodge is one of the largest copper companies in the world and is a community-minded organization, promoting the beautification of cities through gardening and growing.

Here are a few other ideas you can try: Place a peony ring around your rose and see if you don't get a layer plant. Do the same for small evergreens and shrubs to give them a better start.

To keep rabbits and other varmints away from your cabbage patch and charge the air at the same time, make a wire hut over your cabbage and other plants. This will keep your furry friends out and the electric energy in.

Tomatoes can be improved by training them to grow on metal poles rather than wooden stakes. Tie them with nylon strips, made from discarded panty hose, which attracts static electricity. Ask any panty hose wearer about the "static cling."

A BODY'S WORTH

Broken down into its basic chemical parts and sold commercially, the human body, the shell in which even the worst snobs dwell, would bring less on the open market than the same number of pounds of scrap iron or a couple of cases of returnable king-size, soft drink bottles.

Even with inflation, an average-size person would be worth

about three dollars. The body of a man weighing one hundred and sixty pounds contains these main components:

Enough fat for ten bars of soap; carbon for nine thousand pencils; sugar for two cups of coffee; phosphorus for two thousand match heads; chlorine to disinfect five swimming pools; water for one bath; iron for one six-penny nail; sulphur to rid one dog of fleas; lime to whitewash a chicken coop, and enough glycerine to explode one five-inch navy shell.

Manage Your Garden with Perennials

Planting is a perennial project around the garden, year in and year out. The Green Thumb enthusiasts must decide how to fill in the vacant spots under trees and between the evergreens and shrubs. In some cases it seems like a never-ending chain of decisions, but you can put an end to a perennial project by planting perennials. Too many older and more experienced gardeners have forgotten or overlooked the beauty and benefits of the low-cost, fast-growing, colorful perennials. Many of the younger home gardeners have not yet discovered the advantages of these permanent garden residents.

Perennials are the most versatile plant group we have. They can be used as border planting, ground covers, screen planting and cut flowers, in shady areas and wet spots. There are short perennials, tall perennials, fat ones and skinny ones, red ones, blue ones and every color of the rainbow. They can be planted as soon as the soil thaws and any time in between. You can purchase perennials in small plastic bags for as little as a quarter each or in *papier-mâché* pots, tin cans or large bushel baskets. A twenty-five cent investment now can yield you a 500 percent return on investment next season.

We talk about the rose as the Queen of the Garden, and the spruce tree as the Sentinel, while the birch tree is the official Greeter. Now, I would like to introduce you to the Boss of the Garden—the delphinium (Deek). The well-dressed Deek delphinium stands the tallest—in some cases seven feet.

There are three basic types of perennials, determined by the root structure: fibrous (chrysanthemum), fleshy (poppy), and rhizome (iris).

Perennial plants live through the winter and come up year after year. They become larger and more beautiful every season. By combining perennials with different blooming periods you can create beautiful beds and borders in assorted colors that will be in bloom from early spring until killing frost. The designs of perennial beds are almost limitless and may be enlarged or reduced to fit individual tastes and the space available. Tall plants are usually placed in the background of a perennial bed to create a mass effect with medium- and low-growing perennials in the foreground. Plant large groups of three or four plants of the same variety at several locations through the garden to achieve a bold, mass color effect. Don't be afraid to transplant perennials as often as necessary to keep your garden or border looking its best at all times. During the spring and fall, plants can be shifted successfully if you move some soil with the roots.

Perennials can be planted in the spring or fall. Unpack plants immediately upon arrival. If weather conditions are unfavorable, store the plants by potting in moist soil and place in cool basement or garage until they can be planted outdoors in their permanent locations. Dig a hole large enough to accommodate all the roots without crowding and set perennials to the depth recommended on the package.

Since perennials are planted only once and are permanent, it is important that the bed or border be properly prepared to provide good soil in which the roots can easily become well-established. Cultivate the soil to a depth of at least one foot. While perennials can be grown in a wide variety of soils, most perennials thrive best in rich, moist soil.

Some plants, however, will grow in dry as well as moist spots. To improve the soil texture, mix with manure, peat moss, compost, or gypsum. To improve soil fertility, add two pounds of a well-balanced, all-purpose chemical fertilizer such as 4-12-4 or 5-10-5 per hundred square feet and spade it into the soil. It is a good idea to keep the perennial border narrow enough to work easily from both sides. If only one side is accessible, keep the border about forty-two inches wide so you can reach it from one side. Choose your perennial varieties to create a border or bed that will be in bloom all summer.

If possible, lay out the perennial garden to get the benefit of the full sun most of the day, since most perennials require lots of sunshine. If part or all of your bed must be in partial shade, choose varieties that do well under these conditions. For best results, perennials should be mulched after the ground freezes in the fall with a porous mulch that will permit proper air circulation. Once planted, perennials need little care and the plants will bloom year after year. Perennials can be planted at any time except when the ground is frozen, but it is best to plant them in early spring or late fall so that they can become established while the soil is still cool and moist.

HEART OF THE MATTER

A heart attack is nature's way of telling us to slow down. Are you a candidate for a heart attack? First, you should acquaint yourself with what the American Heart Association feels are the signs of a potential heart attack victim:

1. High blood pressure.

2. A history of brief, short-lived "strokes."

3. A variety of heart abnormalities which can be detected by medical examination and x-ray.

4. Evidence of hardening of arteries in other parts of the body, particularly the neck and legs.

5. Diabetes.

6. Increased levels of blood cholesterol and other fats.

7. Cigarette smoking.

8. High levels of red blood cells.

9. The presence of gout.

According to heart expert Dr. Irvine Page of Cleveland, the profile of just the opposite person—the fellow least likely to have coronary disease—would read:

An effeminate municipal worker or embalmer, completely lacking in physical and mental alertness, without drive, ambition, or competitive spirit, who has never attempted to meet a deadline of any kind.

A man with poor appetite subsisting on fruits and vegetables, laced with corn and whale oil, detesting tobacco and spurning ownership of radio, TV and motor car. He has a full head of hair and is scrawny and unathletic in appearance; yet he is constantly straining his puny muscles with exercise.

He is low in income, blood pressure, blood sugar, uric acid, and cholesterol. He has been on nicotinic acid, pyridoxine, and long-term anticoagulant therapy ever since his prophylactic castration.

Paint with Posies

Everyone has some creative talent—be it painting, sculpturing, woodcarving, candlemaking, sewing or music. You, too, are among the "everyones," with this talent for creating. It's merely a question of which and when—*which* field you are talented in and *when* it will appear. Let's begin with *when.* You show others that you, too, can create a masterpiece right now—this coming spring. And the *which*-field question is obvious, considering who is writing this book. You are going to create the most beautiful and spectacular floral display in your neighborhood.

The days may still be cloudy and gray and a little on the chilly side, but April showers will soon warm up the earth and things will begin to pop from below. You had better make your plans on paper now, showing what goes where in the flower beds. The accent is going to be on annuals first, perennials second, bulbs third.

First things first. Careful preparation of the soil is the most important ingredient for creating the spectacular display you are offered. Begin by using a "bow rake" on the soil surface to gather up all of the debris. Pull up last year's dead flower stalks, adding them to the compost pile along with the debris, as we will be using it later on this season for organic food during the hot spell. Next spread fifty pounds of peat moss, twenty-five pounds of gypsum and twenty-five pounds of garden food (4-12-5 or 5-10-5) for every hundred square feet of flower

garden or border (three feet by thirty-three and one-third feet
equals one hundred square feet). Now spade it under to a depth
of eight inches to a foot and smooth out the bumps and lumps,
removing any sticks, stones and glass that might have surfaced
during the spading (do not add wood, wire or glass to the
compost pile).

If you are going to start your annuals from seed, begin now.
The new even-seed flower tapes by Union Carbide will make the
job easier this year, saving you the time and effort in thinning.
If you are going to use the pie-grown plants from the greenhouse, then you will wait until the threat of frost is past. If raw
seed or the seed tapes are used, lay sheets of newspaper two
thicknesses alongside the rows, but not covering them. This acts
as a weed barrier if the bedding plants are used. Cut small holes
in the paper and plant through. Cover the newspaper with fine
wood chips which will act as mulch, in addition to their natural
beauty. Once the flowers are well on their way, sprinkle one of
the garden weeders over the mulch to destroy any stray weeds
wandering into the flower bed.

When new seedlings are about one-inch high, feed them with
one of the fish emulsions. Bedding plants are also fed with fish
emulsion a couple of days after planting, continuing every three
weeks. Insects can be controlled with the normal three-week
shampoo that we use on the rest of the garden. If a flying insect
continues to harass your floral display, add a touch of malathion to your spray. If soil insects are the problem, apply
chlordane to the soil. Once you have planted your annual
flowers and they have broken ground, you can then place your
summer flowering bulbs in the ground, followed by perennials.

The design you use and the color combinations should reflect
your personality and taste. Do not be influenced too much by
professional opinions, but rely on your own imagination.

Has anyone ever seen a genuine Sterling Hayden?

The English Channel has lousy TV shows.

A GARDEN

A garden is a sanctuary, a place set apart wherein flowers, trees and shrubs live together in beauty and harmony.

A garden is hummingbirds, bees and lacy spider webs moistened by the early morning dew.

A garden is pink wiggly worms and pretty butterflies that flit aimlessly from blossom to blossom.

A garden is children and dogs and cats and chirping birds that warn of impending danger.

A garden is rich brown earth, baked warm by the heat of the sun—stones, and bits of twigs and weeds that persist in growing under any conditions.

A garden is high winds and balmy breezes—gentle rain and violent thunderstorms.

A garden is the clean, fresh smell of mother earth after the storm is over.

A garden is a repository for hopes and dreams, disappointments and aspirations.

A garden is today, tomorrow and many yesterdays.

A garden is a beautiful vision to the eye, a potpourri of fragrance to the nose and God's greatest gift to the soul.

THINGS YOU MAY NOT KNOW

The albatross used to be known as "Cape Sheep" apparently because sailors sometimes used their skins as rugs.

According to experiments, bees recognize honey-yielding flowers first by color, and secondly by scent.

A cat's jaw, unlike that of a dog, moves only up and down and not sidewise.

"Blind as a bat" is a meaningless phrase. Contrary to popular belief, most bats can see perfectly well in bright light.

It is untrue that the ostrich hides its head in the sand when confronted by danger. It kicks viciously when cornered or wounded.

Fill the Bill
with Flowering Shrubs

Two of the things most homeowners are interested in today are ways to save money and time. I am deluged with mail asking me to recommend planting selections and suggestions that will give gardeners the most for their money and not require a lot of maintenance. There is an easy and pleasant answer. I simply suggest that they focus their attention on the shrub family, both flowering and foliage.

Shrubs are inexpensive, almost carefree and offer the greatest variety. They produce flowers from early spring until the snow flies, and cover a large area with fewer plants than any other group in Mother Nature's kingdom. There are shrubs for damp spots, wet spots, shaded areas, full sun, clay soil, sand and, yes, even gravel. There are shrubs for privacy screens, hedges, group plantings or ones that look beautiful just standing alone. There are shrubs that provide flowers, foliage, fruit and willow beauty when they are bare of leaves in the winter snows.

In order to have the results I have described, you must take a few precautions. First, ask yourself what you expect your shrub to do. For instance, if you wish to direct traffic you would not ask a flowering almond to withstand the onrush of homeward-bound school children. That's a job for Mr. Barberry (he is qualified and more to the point). You wouldn't ask my good and fragrant friend, Miss Lilac, to absorb a damp situation you had in a low spot. After all, she prefers high ground. That damp job is best handled by the red twig dogwood.

You must use discretion in your selection, planning before you plant. Make a rough layout on a brown paper bag, designing the areas in which you wish to plant. Make sure you mark all of the existing plants, trees, evergreens, etc. This will assist the nurseryman in helping you select the proper shrub to do the job you have in mind. The necessary information that you need to know about each plant—soil condition, light exposure, drainage, maximum height and width at full growth—can be found on attached tags accompanying each shrub.

Flowering shrubs, like their friends the evergreens, are found at the local garden centers in plantable containers (paper pots) and in ball and burlap. Like the rose, shrubs are available packaged (this is the least expensive). The balled-in-burlap shrub will generally be a large and mature plant, while those in containers are of medium growth. Bare-root or packaged shrubs are very young plants. Economics and your personal impatience will dictate your selection. As a rule, the bare-root stock or packaged shrub will grow to maturity within two years, so a little patience can provide you with additional savings.

As with any plant, it is necessary for shrubs to be planted the same day they are purchased. Follow my usual recommended instructions for planting:

1. Dig the planting hole twice as large as, and one inch deeper than, the one in which the plant was growing at the nursery.

2. Add one handful of bone meal and two handfuls of gypsum to soil when planting.

3. Cover soil with two or three layers of newspaper and cover with mulch.

4. Spray newly planted shrubs with mild plant solution to discourage insects from visiting.

Do not confine your selection of shrubs to just those bearing flowers. I highly recommend the use of fruit-bearing shrubs, such as blueberries and gooseberries, to give you additional benefits. If you follow these few simple rules, you can enjoy shrubs for very little cost in either time or money.

THE ALLERGIC GARDENER

Hay-fever sufferers have told me, "Some of my best friends are gardeners." Even if their eyes are red, their noses running, and their spirits low, allergic people can get back to nature if they're careful, consult an allergy specialist and follow his advice.

The study of pollens has become so sophisticated I believe the United States' most important cause of chronic disease, allergy, is losing its mystery and its misery. Immunology is the study that's revolutionizing hay-fever and the like.

Let's take a reminder look at the seasonal and year-round pollens that cause allergies.

The eucalyptus tree spreads its misery from January through September. March, April and May are particularly rough periods for those allergic to sycamore, English walnut and live oak.

In the grasses, Bermuda can keep you down from March through November. April and May are the toughest grass months, generally, with pollen from fescues, rye and Kentucky blue keeping your eyes watering. Johnson grass hits a little later in the year during May through August.

Weeds of all types pollute your allergies, starting in May and running through October. Ragweed's worst two months are August and September.

Sometimes what you blame on flowers, trees, weeds and grass, may be the fault of other things in the environment. The most common year-round environmental allergy-producers are cat hair, cattle hair, chalk, dog hair, glue made from animals, horse hair, house dust, newspaper, sheep wool, tobacco and feathers.

Foods that are most often the allergy-producers are: wheat, celery, chicken, cow's milk, chocolate, eggs, oranges, peanuts, strawberries, tomatoes and cantaloupe.

Flowering Shrubs Serve a Purpose

I am certain that sometime in your life you have been given some advice which contained this phrase: "You should have a purpose or goal in life!" In my case, these words of wisdom fell on deaf ears, primarily because of the age at which I was so advised. After all, at sixteen you are as smart as you are ever going to get, right? At sixteen we know everything, and need no one to tell us anything! But I soon discovered the meaning of the phrase "a purpose in life."

As a youngster I worked with a scratching crew, hoeing weeds in a large nursery. My foreman and teacher was an Indian named Brave Heart who gave me all kinds of the dickens for hoeing too close under an azalea. Don't disturb "the old folks," he said, as they are fulfilling their "purpose in life."

Old folks? Purpose in life? All I could see was five acres of flowering shrubs. But Brave Heart went on to explain that flowering shrubs are called the "old folks" of the garden because they make next spring's flowers on old wood—last year's wood, that is. He went on to explain their whole purpose in life was to bloom and bring health, beauty and fragrance to the world, just like the salmon swimming miles upstream to spawn. It is Mother Nature's way.

The flowering shrub is, when you think about it, the best friend a gardener has. First, they are by far the most beautiful, fragrant and surely the least expensive. The flowering shrub takes the least amount of care, adapts to almost any location, and gives you the most for your money, not to mention the assortment of colors, sizes and shapes. They give so much and ask so little, yet are being overlooked, dug out and removed by gardeners who want a no-maintenance garden.

Hear ye, fellow Green-Thumbers, don't disturb the old folks. With all of the financial and economic news about the squeeze on our pocketbooks, we had best take a look at the benefits of retaining, maintaining and increasing our blooming friends.

When you select a flowering shrub, the first thing you want to know is when it blooms. You don't want them all to bloom at once; spread out the lovely color. Next, what color will the flower be? Don't fill your entire yard with one color, which will eventually bore you. Mix up the colors to fit your fancy. Mother Nature doesn't know what clash means. Find out if it has attractive foliage after blooming, which is yet another plus.

Still we go on. Some of our old friends not only have beautiful blooms, foliage and fragrance, but many offer berries and fruit—some edible, others ornamental. Wait, I'm still not done. There are those, such as blueberries and red twig dogwood, that offer winter beauty with an attractive stem even when they are barren of foliage.

The uses of shrubs are as impressive as the benefits. Let's begin with their ability to serve as a privacy screen for the busy outdoor areas—patio, swimming pools, children's play areas and dog runs. I have made smaller homes look twice and three times as long by adding a row of shrubs on both sides. I have made big, square homes look warm and interesting by breaking up the sharp corners.

Several of our taller shrubs can be used as stand outs, yet they can be planted close together and trimmed into a hedge. Dogwood, some lilacs, common witch hazel, crape myrtle, honeysuckle, spice bush and forsythia are just a few offering this choice.

There are still more uses for flowery shrubs. The low grower can be used to give a finished look to taller plants or can be used as ground covers, as well as low hedges, dividing play areas where a view is necessary to watch small children. In these spots a few examples are: rock cotoneaster, Japanese holly, Oregon grape and dwarf cranberry bush.

Let's review a few things I have previously suggested. Read catalogs and planting labels to find out how tall and wide your choice will grow. Check into the amount of sun, drainage and soil texture it requires. Do not plant acid-loving plants in the same bed as plants that require neutral soil conditions. The reason is obvious: someone is going to get left out.

Don't get carried away and overplant. If you have studied, you will know the size at maturity, so leave plenty of room to grow. Shrubs grow at a rapid rate, which allows you to buy smaller sizes than you would normally be happy with in the evergreen family. Suit yourself and let your budget be your guide. You can purchase shrubs in plastic pacakges, tin cans, burlap balls, *papier-mâché* containers, and so on. I have no preference. Plant them just as soon as you have a realistic plan and you can get a shovel into the ground. But, don't fail to plant them the day you bring them home and in a hole twice as big around as necessary, but only one inch deeper than they were originally planted (plus two inches of wood chips for a mulch).

Don't be afraid to ask questions. Nurserymen are known as talkers and welcome your interest. Their knowledge can mean the difference between success and failure for both you and your plants, so speak up, but be warned: nurserymen can talk the ears off an elephant.

Let's turn to the existing members of our garden—the flowering shrubs that have been there for some time. What can you do to help them? You can begin by giving them an early shower with soap and water. Next, you can dormant-spray them as soon as the weather permits, then place about two inches of dark mulch on the soil beneath, at which time you might spread moth crystals on the soil and mulch to destroy borers and other soil insects.

Flowering shrubs are not really fussy when it comes to eating. They like any low-nitrogen fertilizer, once in early March before bloom time and in June after they bloom.

The real secret to success with flowering shrubs is knowing when to prune them and where not to. Cut all the bouquets you want, especially on lilacs. Do not let them die on the vine. After the shrubs have finished blooming, then, and only then, trim them into the shape desired.

Soap and water should be your only preventative spray. Insecticides will only be necessary when a problem is evident, at which time you should isolate the problem, identify it and apply the chemical or chemicals recommended at the proper rate for the period recommended and no longer.

No one, but no one, can ever say that you don't get your money's worth with flowering shrubs. Try 'em, you'll like 'em.

MAKE FREEWAYS SAFEWAYS

What's the use of all this lovely nature around us if we can't get there alive to enjoy it? Urban travel can literally kill you before you get into the rural area.

As I travel about this great land, more and more I find myself on those concrete thoroughfares known as freeways, where we zip along at maximum speeds, maximum emotions and maximum dangers.

Once you pull onto a freeway, and invariably you will if you hit the road for vacation travel, think of yourself entering an immediate "contract" with motorists in front, behind and to both sides of you. You are committed to them and their movements in what highway department officials call "formation driving."

This "contract" driving also is called "defensive" driving. No matter what it's called, we have to abide by it if we plan to get back to nature. Here are ten tips for turning freeways into safeways:

1. Concentrate on the roadway ahead of you—be ready for such things as blown tires, locked brakes, sudden swerves or lane changes by others.

2. Be aware that drinking drivers may be nearby. Allow plenty of space between you and any vehicle which is speeding or behaving erratically. They are easy to spot. Always avoid blocking his "temporarily insane" moves or responding emotionally. Never let a drunk driver anger you.

3. Never stop on a freeway. If you have a flat or a breakdown, get off the road. If you miss your off-ramp, proceed to the next one—never slow up at the last instant and change direction.

4. When you are in the fast lane, always make way for anything coming up behind, no matter at what speed you are driving. Move over safely, but swiftly.

5. Do not fix your eyes on the white line or any one thing as this limits your peripheral vision. Avoid tunnel vision by keeping your eyes moving to adjacent lanes front and rear, by changing lanes occasionally and changing your speed.

6. When entering a congested freeway, pick your opening quickly, bring your vehicle up to the speed of traffic flow and merge smoothly. Don't come to a stop before entering the freeway. If you don't move out smoothly, other drivers cannot take appropriate action. Spot your opening, signal, accelerate if necessary—and go!

7. Never slash across freeways diagonally; if you plan to use a faster lane, use proper communication and cross the freeway lane by lane in a planned manner.

8. If the car ahead of you spins out of control, don't try to go around him. Aim where he is and if he's skidding, the only place you're sure he won't be two seconds later is where he is right now.

9. If a vehicle comes slamming through the divider on a collision path, your brakes probably won't save you. Swerving to the open spot on your right won't help—that's where he's headed. The feasible alternative is to drive into the center strip,

the place you see the accident vehicle coming from. That's the place he'll leave vacant.

10. Don't demand your legal rights if this might set up a conflict—yield the right of way. Don't trust others to behave courteously. You should be constantly alert to other traffic—the aged and infirm, foolhardy juveniles, unsafe vehicles or intoxicated drivers. Most of all, be alert to yourself and pay attention to and concentrate on what you are doing.

I Can Promise You a Rose Garden

Americans' favorite flower, by far, is the rose. They write more songs about it, compose more poems to its beauty, capture its portrait constantly and send its loveliness as a message of love. We truly put the rose on a pedestal, and well we should, as she is the Queen of the Garden. But like most queens she demands a great deal of attention. To keep her looking her regal best, one must be prepared to spend a little time tending the garden court where she abides.

I have found the reason most folks have trouble growing roses is that they do one of two things wrong. First, they over-care for them—they water them too much, feed them too much too often, prune them too severely, over-dose and over dowse them with garden chemicals. Roses can be killed with kindness. The second reason is obvious—total neglect. This type of gardener simply digs a hole, crams the rose plant in and says you're on your own.

The truly successful "rosarian" is a middle-of-the-roader, giving all the attention necessary to keep Rose looking her best. But should you spoil her, the rest of the members of your garden will become jealous, and what little more performance you get from the rose will be lost by the rest of the flowers.

Here is a middle-of-the-road, rose-care program that should yield you the maximum effort from your roses, without a lot of extra work on your part.

Begin by using common sense in buying. Look the rose bush over carefully and make sure that you have three or more canes, not broken, scarred or nicked (large gouges through the bark on the lower third of the bush). Scrape off the heavy, green, wax coating to see that the wood beneath is moist and green. Avoid plants with a great deal of brownish, black wood, unless you are buying them as bargains at bargain prices.

Next, you can plant roses in April as soon as you can work the soil. Roses will grow in almost any type soil, but do best in a medium, well-drained soil. A good all-purpose mix would be one-third sandy loam, one-third clay loam and one-third peat moss. To this add a handful of steamed bone meal per bush. When healing-up your roses in the fall, this is the mix to use. Do not scoop it from around the roses, but rather bring the soil from somewhere else.

Sunlight plays the biggest part in the survival of roses. You must place your roses in a bright location where they will get at least five hours of sun—morning sun is the best, east and south will give you some real winners. Make sure there are no large tree roots in the area as these will rob your plants of food.

When planting new roses, dig a very wide hole deep enough to bury the large "knot" (graft) one inch below the soil surface. Above all else, read and follow the instructions which are illustrated on each package.

Remove the rose from the package and discard the material in which it was packed. Do not add it to your rose garden soil.

Next, soak the roots in a bucket of warm water with a small amount of tea, for at least two or three hours. Before planting, prune the new rose to stimulate growth. The true secret to success is where you cut. To insure a full, branching plant you are to cut the cane off just above the lowest outside sprout. In many cases this will mean removing two-thirds of a yard or more of the wood, which disturbs most home gardeners, but never fear.

Feeding of roses seems to be misunderstood, but shouldn't be. With the many, many brands of rose food on the shelves today, you should have no trouble. Feed a handful in May, July and August.

Watering is as important as feeding and should be on a regular basis. Water from the bottom to a depth of two inches per week. If rain does the job for you, so much the better.

Insect control can be maintained by dormant-spraying early in the spring, followed with a soap and water bath every couple of weeks. If a problem arises, go to an all-purpose rose spray. Plant garlic or onions between each rose to control aphids and your bug problem should be nil.

To help speed up the rose production of your plants, whenever you cut a rose always snip it off just above a five-leaf cluster. This is where the new flowering shoot will come from. Remove all spent blooms when they no longer look attractive.

To control the weeds, cover the soil with two thicknesses of newspaper overlaid with a mulch of your choice.

These few simple hints can mean the difference between success and failure.

THE "DON'T YOU WORRY" TOWN

There's a town called the "Don't You Worry"
On the banks of the "River Smile"
Where the "Cheer-Up" and "Be Happy"
Blossom sweetly all the while.

Where the "Never-Grumble" Flower
Blossoms beside the fragrant "Try"
And the "Never-Give-Up" and "Patience"
Point their faces toward the sky.

In the Valley of Contentment
In the province of "I Will"
You will find the lovely City
At the foot of "No-Fret-Hill."

There are thoroughfares delightful
In this very charming town
And on every hand are shade trees
Named the "Very-Seldom-Frown."

Rustic benches quite enticing
You'll find scattered here and there
And by each vine is clinging
Called the "Frequent-Earnest-Prayer."

Everyone in town is happy
And is singing all the while
In the town of "Don't-You-Worry"
On the banks of the "River Smile."

—Anon

HOE! HOE! HOE!

Gardeners all know this: it ain't the heat, it's the whew-midity!

You know the garden is going to lose when you swap the seed catalogs for road maps.

Nothing changes a man's line of thought more than digging for fishing worms when you started out spading the garden.

Lawn-mowing husband to lawn-watering wife: "That's right—egg it on!"

Annual
Evergreen Program

Evergreens are the frosting on the landscape cake. When properly placed and cared for, evergreens flatter, hide, guide, protect and enhance your home, patio, play area, animal run and many objects or obstacles that might otherwise cause you much aggravation.

The big problem with evergreens begins with the proper selection and placement. The next problem to crop up is soil condition and maintenance, followed by insect and weather damage (winter kill).

Let's begin this year's program with a little review. This acts as a reminder that whenever you start from scratch or add to your present landscape design you must plan ahead—on paper. Next do a little research to find out just what each plant needs and what it can expect when it comes to live at your home. Then decide whether or not you have the time and patience to tend to their needs and wants. Last, and most important, plant the evergreens the day you bring them home.

Evergreens can be planted as soon as you can completely get a shovel into the ground—that is to say, with only a minimum of effort on your part. This is usually the period from April to November.

The type of container makes no difference, balled in burlap, potted or in tin cans. When you receive them from the garden center they are relatively healthy and happy and it is your responsibility to keep them that way. No matter which you select, remember to dig a "$5 hole for a fifty-cent plant," meaning to dig it twice as wide as necessary, but only one and one-half inches deeper than it was grown in the nursery.

Plant evergreens in a good loose soil, mix about 25 to 30 percent gravel with ordinary topsoil for best results.

Feed all evergreens with a good, old-fashioned garden food in early March (4-12-4, 5-10-5, etc.) to get the roots growing. In May, feed them with an evergreen food or a good lawn food, but don't feed after August 15 with a high-nitrogen food.

Gently clean out over-wintering debris from under the evergreens in early April, lifting up the bottom branches, so as not to break them. Check for mice damage and sterilize the injured area (two tablespoons of household ammonia per quart of water). This same solution is used any time you find an injury on any woody plant or any time you cut on woody plants. Follow this solution with a pruning paint to seal off the wound, preventing entrance of bugs and disease. By hand, pull up all the weeds under and around the evergreens, then apply one of the chemical garden weeders. Lay two layers of newspaper over the soil and cover with wood chips or stone mulch.

Give the evergreens a good soap and water bath in early April (one ounce of liquid green Palmolive in 15 gallons of water). Make sure you get the shower inside, under and over; continue these showers each month (after the first shower of the season, spray with a light application of malathion).

Begin your trimming in May after the new growth has begun. Make sure you do not trim toward the trunk as this will shade the lower area and cause needles to drop.

If signs of damage appear on the foliage shortly after spring, check the soil for insects, apply 44 percent chlordane.

In light soil, water every other day to a depth of six to eight inches; in heavy soil, once a week may be sufficient.

Gypsum should be added to heavy soil around evergreens at a rate of four cups per evergreen.

Feed late in fall with bone meal and a handful of low-nitrogen garden food.

Shampoo in November for the last time, adding a pinch of malathion to discourage any "over-wintering" insects.

Tie up the tall evergreens with pieces of nylon stocking or panty hose, at shoulder, waist and knee heights.

Wrap up any evergreens that will be exposed to west or south winds with burlap to avoid winter kill.

EXIT LINES AND EPITAPHS

I've often wondered what plants and trees would say as their last, dying words.

> *"Don't cut me down!"*
> *"Why didn't you spray more?"*
> *"Water ... water ... water."*
> *"Something's bugging me."*

I'm sure their words would reveal the way we've treated them.

I've been fascinated with the famous last words that have lasted down through the years. These and tombstone epitaphs are interesting, and often immensely personal and profound.

When Ben Franklin was dying, an attendant told him to change position to breathe easier. Franklin said it for us all: "A dying man can do nothing easy."

Author H.G. Wells, whose death lingered, had final words that matched his big ego. He said, "Is there anything in the papers about me?"

Franklin D. Roosevelt's last uttered words were, "I have a terrific headache."

W.C. Fields is reportedly the "author" of more last words than a hundred other dying wits. In all probability, Fields may have said, "Blank 'em all," as it was his favorite response to everything.

Sam Rayburn, the famous Texan who was Washington's Mr. Speaker of the House for years and years, probably uttered the best last words of them all: "This is the damnedest thing that has ever happened to me." And it was.

Dean Martin swears he wants his tombstone epitaph to read: "I told them I was sick."

Douglas Fairbanks, Sr., Tyrone Power and John Barrymore share the same one, a famous line from *Hamlet:* "Good night, sweet prince."

There have been some classics passed down through the years, such as this one supposedly in Tombstone, Arizona:

Here lies Lester Moore
Four slugs from a .44
No les—No Moore.

Many famous people have been asked to write their own epitaphs. Most chose to be humorous. Ernest Hemingway suggested his should read: "Pardon me for not getting up."

It was Seth Parker who requested this one: "Planted, but not yet sprouted."

Joe E. Lewis, who packed several lifetimes into one tragedy-plagued one, wrote his own: "If I had my life to live over again, I wouldn't have the strength to do it."

Ilka Chase wrote her own inscription: "I've finally gotten to the bottom of things."

Oscar Wilde wanted this on his tombstone: "He loved his fellow man."

Tennessee Ernie Ford suggests his own: "Here rests a pea-picker, a-sleeping in his pod. He spent a wondrous life before he hit the sod."

George Bernard Shaw offered a delightful epitaph: "I knew if I stayed around long enough something like this would happen."

Robert Benchley's noted wit would have been on his grave-marker: "This is all over my head."

What would you write for your own epitaph?

Frankenstein sure got it all together.

Summer Care of Evergreens

With the arrival of warm weather, we have a tendency to forget the needs of our good garden friends, the sentinels of our garden—the evergreens. We are too busy keeping the lawn mowed and watered, the roses pruned and cleaned. We take it for granted that the evergreens will take care of themselves. This isn't so. Evergreens react just like a person who is ignored: they begin to pout, and are highly susceptible to insect damage and disease.

If you plan to add new evergreens to your present landscape or are starting from scratch, it is essential you start off on the right foot with your evergreens. Evergreens have their likes and dislikes which never change. The homeowner can start out with a big mistake when he plants his first evergreen, if he looks for the thickest, richest black soil in which to plant his prize. All evergreens prefer light well-drained soil and are grown in the nursery in sand and gravel. Their feeder roots are like fine hair and they like to roam and ramble. I recommend a mixture of 40 percent regular top soil, 20 percent peat moss and 40 percent sharp sand or gravel, plus two liberal handfuls of gypsum, to fill the hole when planting evergreens.

The second mistake made is not digging the hole large enough. Since evergreens like to spread out roots and tops, it is a good idea to give both the room to do so.

The next common error is not planning ahead. Young evergreens, like young people, do not always stay the same size.

When my wife buys clothes for our young son, she buys a half-size larger to accommodate his growth.

When you plant evergreens, find out how large they will grow and then plant them far enough apart and away from walls to let them attain normal size. Overplanting seems to be a major problem. Remember, the number of evergreens you use depends upon the desired landscape effect. Landscape design should complement the home, not compete with it.

Think of major plants, such as evergreens, as guests that are going to stay a long while. Find out what they like and dislike, and you will make their visit happy and long-lived:

Pines, spruces and firs prefer full sun and extremely light soil, while yews and Canadian hemlock will thrive in medium shade on the north side of a building.

Junipers like full sun, but will also do nicely in light shade. It is best to use broad-leaf evergreens, such as azaleas, rhododendrons, pieris, japonica, holly and mountain laurel, in damp shady spots and use needle-leaf evergreens in sunny areas.

Evergreens have the proverbial "hollow leg" when it comes to water. They like a lot to drink, but not to stand in. Water evergreens deeply twice a week through the summer, but do not allow them to stand in water or they will actually drown.

Your guest has a healthy appetite and will eat the same food you feed the grass, as long as it does not have weed killers in it. Feed evergreens at a rate of half a pound per foot of height in April and June. Never feed evergreens after August 15, as you will stimulate abnormal new growth and Jack Frost will paint it right out of next year's picture.

Your evergreens will, from time to time, get a little shaggy-looking if not tended. To keep them looking their best, shear them now and then. The best time is when new growth is about one to one and one-half inches long. Shear off half the new growth on yews. On pines, spruces and firs, trim the candles when they are two inches long back to an inch.

Junipers are the fast growers and generally the ones that grow out of proportion first. When the new growth is five or six inches, cut it back to three inches. The same goes for arborvitae (cedar).

When shearing evergreens use only sharp tools and do not slant the trimming design in, as this will not allow the sun to reach all sides of the shrub. When the needles on an evergreen are brown remove them, they will not turn green.

Since evergreens are thick and cool, insects and disease find them a fine place to lodge. It is therefore a mandatory chore to spray regularly. Spray occasionally with a soap and water solution and once a month with a broad spectrum insecticide (spectricide). Sprinkle moth crystals under your evergreens to control soil insects and discourage some dogs and other rodents.

When we talk of evergreens we naturally think of them as all green. But many evergreens have winter and summer color. When planning your landscape take into consideration both summer and winter appearances.

I would suggest that you have at least one or two of these evergreens in your garden where you can look out on a cold winter day and see the warm purple, light blue or vivid orange of the Andora juniper, Hill's Dundee juniper, *Pyracantha,* or *Pieris japonica.*

Planting time is no longer a problem with evergreens as most of them are now in plantable paper containers, plastic containers, burlap wrapping and in cans, and can be planted any time you can dig in the soil.

BUMMERS BEWARE!

As you get back to nature and backpack around the country (we used to call it bumming around), there are some laws I think you should know about.

I must admit these archaic laws, while still on the statute books, are mostly forgotten and unenforced.

You can't sleep in a restaurant in Kentucky for example. In Prescott, Arizona, it is unlawful to ride a horse in a hotel lobby.

In Tulsa, Oklahoma, you aren't allowed to open a pop bottle

in a bar unless a licensed bartender is present. What are you doing drinking pop in a Tulsa bar anyway?

New Jersey bar-goers would be rather amused to know it's against the Garden State's law to chase whiskey with beer. There goes the number one drink in New Jersey—the Boilermaker.

With the bike craze going on, Winter Haven, Florida, cyclists should be warned that it's against the law to pedal a bike while intoxicated. Need we add that it is also a physical impossibility?

Kentucky, where they grow bourbon, has a law that says one is sober until he cannot stand upright. I guess you sit in a chair and get as snockered as you wish.

Nebraska won't even allow a tavern proprietor to sell beer unless there is a kettle of soup cooking on the stove. I'm sure that somewhere there's a law that prevents the sale of soup unless some beer's brewing. Probably in Milwaukee.

In Memphis, Tennessee, if a waitress serves a customer a piece of pie, he must eat it or throw it away. No doggy bags for sweet-toothed canines in Memphis.

As you bum around the country, remember you can't have cherry pie a la mode in Kansas, and Winona Lake, Indiana, restaurants can't serve you ice cream on Sunday.

I'm not sure which five counties in Maryland they are, but there are five where a husband is able to buy a drink at a bar only as long as his wife approves. That may be the most overlooked and unenforceable law in history.

You assume that when these laws were placed on the books they were taken very seriously by the public. I wonder if a couple of decades from now some of the laws presently putting people behind bars in this country may well be as silly as that forbidding ice cream on Sunday.

THINGS YOU MAY NOT KNOW

The elephant is the only mammal that kneels when reclining. His knee joint rests on the ground while his hind foot sticks out backward.

Landscape with Fruit and Nut Trees

When we purchase a product or service we always attempt to get the best quality and quantity for the least investment. It should be the same when we select any addition to our garden. We must get the most out of each plant, and the fruit and nut trees certainly fill the bill. Where else can you get so much for so little? Floral beauty and fragrance in the spring, shade from the foliage, and the payoff is obvious.

But for some reason we fail to recognize all the advantages of standard and dwarf fruit trees, not to mention the nut trees. We tend to forsake these valuable and beautiful trees for the standard shade trees. I am depressed whenever I see a home where the owners have used the standard stereotyped land-scaping, not their own imagination or originality. The proper use of fruit trees can set apart the average and the original.

When using fruit trees in your landscape plan follow the same standard procedure of planning before you plant. That means do not plant over septic tanks, tile fields, sewers or drains. Even though fruit trees do not grow as tall as the maples, elms and oaks, they must not be planted under telephone or electric wires.

Do not plant too close to buildings or under eaves, or your trees will raise the roof. Do not plant within fifteen feet of a drive or walk as they can move concrete if they have a mind to.

For all practical purposes there are four basic-size fruit trees for the home gardener: *Double Dwarf,* which grow approximately six to eight feet tall when full-grown, are particularly suitable for small space, and develop standard-size fruit; *Dwarf*, which grow eight to ten feet tall; *Semi-dwarf*, with general height of twelve to fifteen feet; *Standard*, which grow twenty-five feet tall or more.

You have heard the line from the song that goes: "I can do anything you can do better." Well, this is what the fruit trees say to the shade trees. Your local garden center has many, many varieties. The nut trees will need a great deal more space than the fruit trees, but then they grow a great deal taller and broader.

Here are the general rules for growing and caring for these productive wizards: Standard fruit trees require about twenty feet for proper development, so space them accordingly. Fruit trees should be planted immediately after arrival. Do not allow the roots to become exposed to the air or sun; keep them covered with a damp cloth until planted. Dig the hole large enough so that the roots will not be crowded. Make a separate pile of fertile soil—the first six to eight inches of soil removed. Fruit trees should be planted about two inches deeper than they were grown in the nursery, with the graft or bud union just below the soil level. Trim off any bruised or broken roots. Place the fertile top soil around the roots so there are no air pockets. Fill the hole firmly for two-thirds, then fill the sides to the top, leaving a saucer-like depression to catch the rain. If available, a mulch of well-rotated manure should be used the first year to hold moisture and build fertility. Fertilizer or manure should not come in contact with the roots or trunk. I recommend that all fruit trees be staked and protected against winter weather and gnawing by rodents. Use wire mesh or similar protective material around the base. Tree wrap as recommended to prevent scalding by the sun. Stake by driving a pipe or two-by-two board about six inches from the tree and fasten with a wire loop run through old garden hose.

Dwarf fruit trees have become very popular with home gardeners during recent years for several reasons. Eight dwarf trees can be planted in the space ordinarily occupied by one standard tree, so several different varieties and types can be planted. Dwarf trees grow no higher than you can reach and are easy to spray, prune and care for. The trees bear full-size fruit two years after planting. While dwarf trees don't bear as much fruit as standard trees, more trees can be planted in the same amount of space, making the ultimate crop about equal. Dwarf trees should be planted twelve feet apart using the same steps outlined for standard fruit trees, with one exception: it is very important to place the graft or bud union three to four inches above the soil level. Dwarf trees should be staked at the time of planting to strengthen the graft.

Two important essentials with nut trees are: they must have well-drained soil to survive and must have plenty of room to grow. Plant chestnuts thirty feet and all others forty to fifty feet apart for best results. Plant nut trees the same as fruit trees or shade and flowering trees, except in the case of tap-rooted trees such as walnuts. With such trees dig a U- or V-shaped hole and fill in the soil carefully all the way up over the top and side roots. Stake nut trees securely so that they won't whip about in the wind and keep them well-watered, especially during dry periods. Nuts should be protected from rodent damage as with fruit trees. It is also a good idea to protect these trees from sun-scald the first winter with tree-wrap paper. Nut trees are usually very slow to leaf-out after they are planted, so please be patient. Most nut trees are not self-fertile so be sure to plant two trees for proper pollination. Even nuts have a sex life.

A few varieties of fruit and nut trees either will not bear at all, or will not bear consistently good crops unless they are pollinated with another variety. It is best to purchase two or more varieties of apricot, sweet cherry, chinese chestnut, and English walnut to insure fruiting. All apples, peaches, pears and plums are self-fertile and will bear fruit without cross-pollination; however, it is always advisable to plant more than one variety of the same family of fruit as possible.

The gardener prunes fruit trees to keep the trees thin enough so that they won't break because of a heavy crop of fruit, and high enough to mow and sit under. Young branched fruit trees should be pruned rather severely at the time of planting to form a head. Prune thin, leaving five or seven branches evenly distributed around the stem and cut back the main stem at least one-third. Do not leave any two branches directly opposite each other as they will form a fork where the tree will be likely to split. For all practical purposes side limbs don't get any higher off the ground as the tree matures, so don't leave low limbs unless you just desire a low-branched tree. Following the first season's growth, these headed trees should have the new growth pruned back about one-third. This great sacrifice of wood may seem wasteful but it is essential to the vigor, strength and future productivity of the tree. If thorough pruning is done the first two seasons, very little pruning will be required in succeeding years. Prune apples so they develop a central leader, with alternate side branches; trim peaches so they grow low by cutting back the leader and all side branches; cherries, pears and plums usually don't require any pruning after planting.

In most home-planting, dwarf fruit trees are handled more or less the same as standard trees and should be pruned in a similar manner. When received from the nursery, young apples, pears, peaches, cherries and plums should have excess growth removed, selecting five to seven well-spaced branches that will develop into a strong head. Dwarf trees produce fruit earlier than standard trees and during the first two or three years it is best to remove most of the fruit since excessive production at this time may prevent proper growth of the tree. As the trees mature, regular dormant-pruning should be practiced to maintain the desired size and shape. A regular program of cutting back or heading will increase the production of the short fruiting branches (spurs) which produce the fruit. Dwarf trees are ideally suited for training to grow along fences, walls, trellises and espaliers.

Insect control is not difficult if you will just use a little common sense. First, if your trees are well-fed, pruned properly and damaged wood removed or repaired, odds are the insects will pass you by.

Next, dormant-spray in the late fall and early spring followed with a soap and water shampoo on a monthly basis. If chemical control is necessary, use one of the many home-orchard sprays on the market as directed. Give yourself, your family and your garden a treat and add fruit trees to the floral picture in your yard. You will also give every neighbor and passerby a visual treat, too.

HOW MUCH IS YOUR TIME WORTH?

You should consider each minute and hour as time earned or lost. To put time in its proper perspective, *The Notebook of Solomon Huber* has devised a table which shows just how important your time is in comparison to your income.

The following table shows the value of each hour and minute spent earning your income. It is based on 244 eight-hour working days a year.

IF YOU EARN	ONE HOUR IS WORTH	ONE MINUTE IS WORTH
$ 5,000	$ 2.56	$0.0426
7,500	3.84	$0.0640
8,500	4.35	0.0726
10,000	5.12	0.0852
12,000	6.15	0.1025
15,000	7.68	0.1278
20,000	10.25	0.1708
25,000	12.81	0.2134
35,000	17.93	0.2986
50,000	25.62	0.4268
100,000	51.24	0.8536

A dog is something that's always on the wrong side of the door.

Don't let the Blood Bank get caught with its pints down.

To Have a Good Garden Be a Cut Up

Groundhog Day comes and goes, with the groundhog usually casting a shadow because all the TV camera light crews are on hand. To some of us it means that we don't have to rush around and finish some of the late-winter chores. To others it means six more long weeks of winter weather. To those who get down in the dumps because the groundhog sees his shadow, remember the saying: "Time flies for busy hands." There are many jobs you can do for the garden to make time fly and help you have a better lawn and garden.

In the last couple of years, grapes have become extremely popular! Why grapes? In many newer neighborhoods developers have prohibited fencing, so many ingenious gardeners have turned to the mighty grapevine to control the traffic flow through their yards. It is an excellent choice, giving the width and depth necessary for a screen plant, plus a unique beauty and character. Above all other assets, the fruit of the vine is delicious. You can eat your fence.

The biggest problem most folks run into when they tackle grapes is how to train them. Grapevines must be pruned every year in the middle of February. Grape clusters are formed on new shoots, which break from buds on last year's growth. Year-old branches produce the biggest and best fruit, the largest, healthiest foliage and the strongest support. The big problem is that you get too much of this new growth and it becomes crowded and tangled and very little fruit can form.

The secret? Severe pruning! Make sure that your pruning shears are sharp, just as a surgeon's scalpel. Your sterilizing solution ingredients are two tablespoons of household ammonia per quart of water. Apply it liberally with a paint brush or with an old window spray bottle to any woody-cane plant that you hack, whack, tear, break, pinch or chop. It destroys disease-bacteria and discourages bugs. Next, seal the cuts you make on the grapevine and other woody wonders with asphalt paint. I know several gardeners who say cut-end bleeding won't hurt, but I disagree. It invites serious infections, so I dress all wounds. Now, look over the grapevine and select the four longest branches, two on each side, one above the other. Remove all the rest. When removing excess branches leave one stub, with two buds each, either just above or just below each of the long branches you are using for fruit this year. These stubs will become next year's fruiting branches.

Stretch the long branches out gently and weave them around the wire or fence that will be their support. Tie the ends and middle with small pieces of nylon hose, since this is strong and flexible, yet very gentle on the young bark and foliage. You will get the best foliage and most fruit from branches that have from eight to ten buds each. If the branches have more cut them back.

Make sure you leave some of the small pieces of wood you remove from the vine on the ground to discourage little animals from gnawing on the trunks. Scatter, by hand, a low-nitrogen garden food on the soil surface below or, in the winter, on the snow after pruning.

Next, let's turn our attention to the fruit trees. They are best pruned at the same time as grapes, mid-to-late February. Use the same sharp tools. Nine out of ten problems I come in contact with regarding the lack of fruit on fruit trees are the result of little or no pruning. You can't let an apple, cherry, plum, peach, apricot or pear tree go its own way and expect a bumper crop. Pruning is as necessary as buying children new shoes. If a child's feet become cramped, the growth of the toes is stunted. A crowded branch on a fruit tree will also cramp its style and deform or stop the growth of fruiting spurs. On fruit trees remove all damaged branches, diseased wood or weak shoots. Do not allow suckers to grow at all from below the soil, as they will virtually sap the life out of the tree. Do not permit the tree to get too high or wide. A well-shaped tree is a heavy-bearing tree. Strong and healthy trees will have little or no problem with insects and diseases.

Apples, pears and cherries should be half-mooned. Keep them shaped much as a youngster's head looks when his hair has been cut with a soup bowl over it.

Peaches should be pruned to have two out of three of last year's branches removed on both the vertical and horizontal branches.

Plums make fruit on spurs that grow on the tops of the branches that look much like toes. I cut off end branches that are growing downward and remove all but one new end shoot from a branch.

Feed all of the fruit trees with a garden food as soon as you finish pruning.

DANGERS AFIELD

The only "wild animals" of the outdoors that will make an unprovoked attack on humans are mosquitoes and blackflies. These are the real dangers afield.

Most woodland travelers worry about wolves, bears and snakes, but more people are hospitalized from mosquito and blackfly bites than from the onslaughts of bigger critters.

The mosquito has a longer period of attack on humans—from April until September—in most northern states and Canadian provinces.

The blackfly, fortunately, has a shorter season of attack— from late May until early July. But when he is active, he's a greater menace.

Blackflies have long been suspected of carrying parasites and disease from one animal to another and they have been the subject of a great deal of research. There is no evidence that they are carriers of any human ailment, but for some people their bites can be very painful. Too many bites at once can put some people in a hospital.

Before modern insecticides, it was not unusual for outdoor workers to be driven from the woods during the worst of the "fly season." Today, however, most of the insect repellents will work.

It's a rare human who hasn't been bitten by a mosquito. It has a sting like the jab of a needle. The blackfly, on the other hand, works painlessly.

You know you've been a blackfly's meal when you see fresh blood running down your skin.

Some of them are so small they penetrate some cabin and tent screens, and they have the nasty habit of getting in under your clothing, into your hair or inside your ears and nose.

I tape down my cuffs or tuck them inside boots. Clothing should be buttoned up tight, with a bandanna around the neck for added protection. In the really bad times, gloves help and so does a fine-screen head net.

Keep in mind that dark clothing tends to attract bugs. Wear light-colored garments in fly time. Hair tonic and shaving lotions also seem to attract them.

Remember if you are working around water or handling wet objects like fish (if you're lucky), the moisture will wash away the insect repellent. Reapplications are necessary.

—Jerry Chiapetta

One of the coolest known forms of light is that given off by the firefly.

Trees and Shrubs Are a Solution to Pollution

With the increase in population, we are faced with the congestion of noises, air and water pollution. But most people do not realize that trees can help toward improving our environment, making it more beautiful and livable.

One well-chosen tree, properly placed, contributes in so many ways to the home grounds. Trees are the most important natural asset we have. They add beauty, give shade, serve as a barrier against noises, form windbreaks, screen views, add value to the property and help purify the air we breathe.

There is also a connection between trees and good water supply. Trees and other vegetation control excessive water runoff and erosion. They cover the earth and the surface soil with a system of interlacing roots. Grasses, leaves, decayed twigs, needles and other organics form a spongy blanket above the roots. Aboveground we end up with a natural mulch.

When rain falls on the tree canopy, the force of drops is broken by the leaves and branches. After a heavy rain, the water may trickle down the branches and trunk and drip slowly from the leaves, thereby preventing rain drops from beating soil particles into suspension.

Spongy soil formed by a decayed litter is loosened by root masses and other organisms, allowing water to enter slowly, infiltrating and replenishing the ground water supply. This supplies needed moisture for plant life and finally seeps into lowlands, springs and rivers. The more slowly water travels, the more good it does along the way.

In contrast, we have erosion where we do not have vegetation to stop heavy rains from beating the soil. Erosion is the gradual gnawing away of soils by rain and winds and causes soil runoff. This soil is diverted to ditches, streams, rivers and lakes. Carried away with the runoff are great quantities of soil and chemical wastes. The prevention of excessive runoff and inevitable soil erosion is one of the most important steps in water-pollution prevention.

The clean-up of debris from rivers and lakes, or the dredging of soil from harbors and rivers, and moving this same waste farther from shore is not the answer. Pollution must be stopped at its source and on many fronts. The first front is your front yard. More trees and shrubs must be planted where erosion and soil runoff exist, diverting the rains into the soil and controlling the runoff. This condition exists in suburban areas where we only plant a lawn and no shrubs. We must think as conservationists as well as gardeners and plant trees. This will reduce the millions of tons of soil and wastes from entering our rivers and lakes and polluting our water supply, as well as improve our ecological balance for generations to come.

On one summer day a medium-sized apple tree soaks up about eight hundred pounds, or ninety-four gallons, of water. Leaf pores then give out about 96 percent of the water to the air. You can see why trees are one of our greatest natural resources.

Success in growing shade trees in the city depends most on selecting species tough enough to survive in an unfavorable environment.

Replace poor soil from the hole with good soil, pack well under the roots, and stake or guy the tree before filling in the rest of the soil.

Peat moss, peanut hulls, and wood chips are good mulches for conserving moisture and protecting against extreme heat and cold.

Apartment dwellers! Want a tree on your balcony this summer? Try a Japanese maple, a Hop hornbeam, or Foster holly in a tub.

Well-placed shade trees can reduce summer room temperature of a frame house in an arid climate by as much as twenty degrees.

Water is especially important for a tree's first two growing seasons. It is better to soak trees thoroughly once a week if no rains come than to sprinkle every day.

He that planteth a tree is a servant of God,
He provideth a kindness for many generations,
And faces that he hath not seen shall bless him.

—Henry van Dyke

Secretarial Plant Guide

Secretarial success is measured by the authority commanded by your employer and secondly by the amount of income you receive.

The executive secretary is one of the proudest titles women in general business can have. It is not a position that is easily gained, nor is it a lifetime position. Like any pro, in any field, the executive secretary must constantly improve her game. It is taken for granted that her shorthand and typing are impeccable, that her personal appearance is neat and fashionable, and her personality is pleasant and efficient.

The difference between the super secretarial star and the ordinary player comes in the little extra secrets she has learned on the way up. One of the secrets I refer to is lobby-landscaping and executive-suite ecology—plain, old-fashioned, green-plant care. I have never met a business executive who didn't enjoy the appearance of healthy, flowering green plants in his office and vestibule. It gives him the feeling of elegant success, while putting his visitors in a relaxed mood and adding a breath of fresh air to the cold and sometimes sterile surroundings in many of today's lofty office complexes. Imitation plastic and paper plants and flowers are no substitute and are not appreciated by most successful executives, because they give just the opposite atmosphere.

Since the improvements in architecture, heat and lightning, you can now enjoy virtually any flower or green plant that is available. Up until a few years ago you were restricted to a few of the hearty, but not too attractive, green plants.

A good secretary knows how to select plants that complement her employer's personality, appearance and interior decor of his office. She will know which plants can survive in cool temperatures corresponding with her employer's choice of climate. She knows how to cope with lack of humidity, killing drafts, and dim lighting. A really good secretary develops a Green Thumb and can recognize instantly a plant problem or deficiency and corrects the situation before the condition is called to her attention by her boss or one of his associates. There is nothing more depressing than the appearance of a sick plant or wilted flower that will affect his mood and attitude for the entire day.

If you aspire to be an executive secretary or improve your present position, why not practice a little Green Thumb know-how? The association with the green world can't miss making you a growing success.

To begin your Green Thumb education, learning to select the right plant to fit your employer's personality can develop into quite a challenge. Most men occupying the executive suite got there by hard work, imagination, enthusiasm and plain, old-fashioned guts. They are, for the most part, heavy-hitters and do not like to think that they depend on anyone to support them.

Lesson Number One is don't select a vine-type plant, a fragile fern foliage or delicate flowered plant for the executive suite. This type of plant tends to deflate the male ego. Next group to avoid are the fat pudgy-leafed plants such as *Peperomia* or African violet, even if these plants resemble your employer's stature. To be on the safe side and score points, select any one of the following plants from a purely, personality standpoint: fiddle leaf fig, rubber plant, Rex or Iron Cross begonia, cast-iron plant, parlour palm, umbrella plant, *Cordyline, Monstera, Pandanus* (screw pine), *Philodendron bepinnatifidum,* staghorn fern, *Syngonium* (goose foot), *Aechmea* (urn plant), Chinese evergreens, *Schefflera* (Australian umbrella), variegated Indian rubber tree, *Dracaena* (corn plant). There are hundreds of green plants on the market but those in this limited list are the hardiest and most masculine group of plants, requiring very little attention and any one or a combination will complement most human personalities as the surrounding architectural decor.

None of the tropical plants can live in a cold, dark room for a long period of time. They must eventually have some heat and light. Plants are much like people and any condition that makes you uncomfortable will also be uncomfortable to most plants.

Look the room over carefully and decide which of the following categories best describe the existing conditions: (1) cool and dim, (2) bright but sunless, (3) sunlight part of the day, (4) sunlight most of the day, (5) sunlight all day, (6) little heat in the winter, (7) gas heat, (8) electric heat, (9) steam heat, and (10) poor humidity. Put it all together—your employer's personality, his stature, the growing conditions and decor of the office—to make your selections:

Category 1. Fiddle-leaf fig, rubber plant, variegated Indian rubber tree, Iron Cross and Rex begonia, cast-iron plant, parlour palm, umbrella plant.

Category 2. All plants listed.

Category 3. All plants listed.

Category 4. All plants except the begonias.

Category 5. All plants except the begonias.

Category 6. Fiddle-leaf fig, rubber plant, variegated Indian rubber tree.

Category 7. Fiddle-leaf fig, rubber plant and tree, *Monstera*. (You may select any one of the rest. However, if any immediate signs of drooping appear, call the gas company.)

Category 8. All plants listed.

Category 9. Best condition for both you and all plants.

Category 10. Fig, rubber plant and tree.

Light is the most important thing to keep in mind if you hope to maintain the shape of the plants you select. Too little light will make the plants tall and stringy, while too much light will stunt their growth. The fluorescent lighting in most offices is an excellent source, but is seldom found inside of the executive suites where a more subtle light is preferred. With the exception of Category 1, plants need ten to twelve hours of light per day and no more than fourteen. It is an excellent idea to open the drapes when your employer is out and attach an inexpensive timer to a fluorescent desk lamp for the short winter days.

Watering of the big plants seems to be a problem, but shouldn't be. You water all plants when the surface soil feels dry to the touch, and then do not water again until it feels dry. Use only room-temperature water in which a used tea bag has been steeped unless you are using distilled water. In a very dry office this could mean watering every day. In a more cool, humid office it could mean three times a month.

Feeding should only be done from March to October for your plants, and then with one of the fish emulsions. In the winter months it is a good idea to poke a one-a-day vitamin (the same kind that is used for human consumption) into the soil to give the plants needed trace elements they will miss during the dull winter days.

Humidity is as important to plants and their health as it is to you or me. Green plants need more moist air than warm air. If they lack this added humidity, the foliage will shrink up and fall off. To avoid this, have the plants set on a tray of gravel and keep the water level in the gravel half full, not touching the pot. Next, shower the foliage each morning with an old window sprayer. You might even suggest an attractive aquarium be placed close by so the additional evaporation will add to the humidity and the fish will give the plants someone to talk to.

The perfect office temperature for plants is seventy-two degrees days and sixty-five degrees nights. If these temperatures seem familiar it is because they are the same that are recommended for humans. Plants can catch cold, run a fever, cry tears, and suffer shock from dehydration. When the condition has gone too far they become anemic and they die from shock. Be alert to avoid these conditions.

If the edges turn black or brown the plant is in a draft (hot or cold) and must be moved. If small beads of moisture appear on the top of the leaves it is running a temperature and has caught cold. If the leaves become scaly or crack, dehydration has set in. If you notice the foliage is a pale yellow color and the veins dark green it is anemic.

To cure a plant cold: (1) stop feeding it, (2) cover the soil surface with a layer of plant charcoal, (3) if the soil is dry, water well, or if the soil is damp, do not add more water, but let it dry out to some degree, (4) wash the foliage with a mild solution of soap and water and rinse with mild tea.

If the dehydration has appeared, set the plant in a larger

container with a brick placed in the bottom. Next, pour scalding hot water into the large container and set the plant on the brick. Do not let the hot water touch the plant or pot. Let it set in the steam for five to six minutes and then return to a comfortable draft-free location.

To find a draft-free location simply place a lit candle on a saucer and place on the floor or table where you intend to set the plant. Watch the flame. If it goes out or leaps in one direction for a long period of time you have selected the wrong location. The flame must burn straight or flutter to indicate a suitable draft-free home for the plant.

To improve or stop the anemia, feed the plant with one ounce of Green Garden Micronized Iron found in any garden center. When the plant has recovered and is looking better, dilute a quarter-cup of very flat beer in a quart of water and feed generously.

Give the plants plenty of exercise by having them turned at least a quarter of a turn a week. This will also assure you of their balanced growth. I would insist on plant stands with casters for large, showy plants.

Insect problems can be controlled by spraying the tops and undersides of the leaves with any indoor plant bomb in the late afternoon and by sprinkling a small amount of 6 percent chlordane ant powder on the soil. From time to time plants that are confined to the inside will need a bath with soap and water. This is done to remove surface tension which is caused by dust accumulation on the surface of the foliage and restricts photosynthesis (the plant's natural ability to manufacture its own food). Add one tablespoon of liquid dish soap to two quarts of water and proceed to wash tops and underside of leaves. Rinse and spray foliage with a weak tea solution. If, after all of this concern and effort, you do not get a promotion or a raise, you can always get a job in a flower shop.

Say it with flowers—mums the word.

HERB BEAUTY BATH TEA

Women, bless 'em, are garden-like. They are beautiful in bloom. Like gardens, women always want to look their very best. Believe it or not, gardens are very vain. They really like to look their very best at all times and resent it when you neglect their beauty care.

Because of the many, many requests I've had for this little recipe after mentioning it on my television appearances, I thought it worthwhile to include in an almanac that's full of handy information.

Herb Beauty Bath Tea: Take a half-handful of thyme, rosemary, mint, orange peel and lemon peel. Enclose in a cloth bag. Now let this steep in a hot bath. Lounge in the bath until mixture cools. Your skin will tell you what's happening.

Easter Plants
Can Last for Years

Easter Sunday is the unofficial beginning of spring. It matters ot if it comes in March or April, warm or cool. When the ight array of colorful spring fashions are displayed at Easter time, and the windows of flower shops and roadside stands display their full and colorful panorama of gift plants, spring fever's symptoms are high in the land.

We get the urge to get growing, but often as not it is just a little early to get out-of-doors with an early Easter. However, I have a suggestion for temporary relief. Turn your attention to the care of your recently received holiday plants.

The biggest complaint I hear from recipients of a gift plant is that they don't last long enough. That needn't be the case if a few precautions are taken when the plant is received.

To begin, the colorful, foil wrapping and attractive bows and decorations that cover and surround the pot that the plant has been grown in are for display and decoration only. They are of no benefit and, as a matter of fact, they are a definite danger to the life of the plant if left on long. When you first receive your gift plant, take your finger and poke a hole through the foil wrapping in the bottom of the pot. This allows proper drainage. If it is not done, when you water the plant the excess water would have no way of escaping and your plant would drown. Next, place the plant on a shallow saucer or pie tin filled with small pebbles. This helps to raise the humidity in the vicinity of your plant. After you have displayed your plant for a few days select a temporary home for it in a south, east or north window until it is time to move it outdoors.

Nearly all of the potted gift plants get along nicely at normal room temperatures of seventy degrees during the day. To prolong the flowering time I suggest you move them to a cooler spot in the evening.

When you move them, remove the foil wrapping to let the clay pot beneath breathe. It is not recommended that you feed your gift plant for at least a month. It has had sufficient fertilizer in the greenhouse.

A proper water technique is perplexing to many of you, but it needn't be. Here's my rule of Green Thumb for watering: water well when the soil feels dry to the touch, then do not water again until the soil feels dry. Simple enough.

The exception to this rule is with mums, calceolarias, cine

arias and hydrangeas. These blooming beauties can't seem to get enough water and require a daily quantity. Fill a bucket about half full with tepid water and submerge the whole pot into the water. Remove and drain. Repeat each day.

With a little care and patience you can enjoy your holiday plants not just for days, weeks or maybe a month or two, but for years. Each type of plant has its own personality, its own likes and dislikes. If you pamper them in the beginning, they will soon fend for themselves.

Here is a little background information on a few of the more popular ones.

Chrysanthemums. Your gift mum needs daily watering, and plenty of sunshine. Keep it a little closer to the window as it prefers a little cooler temperature than most of the others. When the threat of frost has passed, cut the foliage all the way back and plant in the garden in a nice, sunny spot.

Calceolarias. This is an old favorite, making a comeback. It's often called Grandma's Pocketbook, because the shape of the flowers are like bright pouches. This plant prefers a cooler temperature, also needs plenty of light, but not direct sunlight. I recommend a north window. Water daily. When flowers begin to wilt and turn color, pinch them off and new ones will appear. Plant in the garden in a light, shady spot, pot and all and return to the house before frost.

Easter Lilies. Place your lilies in the north window, also. Pinch the yellow anthers inside the trumpets as soon as they arrive and remove the blossoms from the plant as they fade. Water when soil is dry and be sure to let the water get all of the way to the bottom. When the plant has died down cut it off and plant in a sunny spot in the garden when the weather warms.

Azaleas. Place your azalea in a bright, but not too strong, sunny window (east should do). Keep the soil evenly moist, maintaining a temperature of fifty-five to sixty-five degrees. Spray the foliage three or four times a week to improve humidity. An old window sprayer is handy for this job. After flowers have disappeared, sink pots and all into the ground in a semi-shade and return to house in early fall.

Tulips and Hyacinths. You will hold the blooms on these plants if you keep them in an eastern exposure and rather cool. Water bulb plants daily. Do not let them dry out or become too warm. I use cool water as opposed to the tepid temperature that the other plants prefer. Plant the bulbs outdoors when the weather will permit and enjoy them for years.

Hydrangeas. This plant has a hollow leg when it comes to water and will need water daily. If your home is kept near seventy-five degrees it will require water twice daily. Place your hydrangea in a north window after the plant has finished blooming. Cut back stems to the pot, plant in a good sunny spot, pot and all. In the fall when you return it to the house cut it all the way back again and water daily. Feed once a week with fish emulsion.

Cyclamen. My favorite. This plant looks out for itself. It will tell you when it wants water. The leaves will turn over when it's thirsty. Water thoroughly. The cyclamen would prefer that you keep a day temperature of seventy degrees and fifty-five in the evenings. Submerge this plant to water it. When summer comes along place on patio in a sunny spot.

ON BEING LOST

You are never lost as long as you are awake.

Your car may be lost or your friends may be lost but a conscious sportsman in a strange woods is never lost as long as his eyes are open.

You may be bewildered for a day or two, but that doesn't mean anything to a guy who can keep his cool.

Contrary to what you might have read before, it is not important that you gather wood, build a fire, build a shelter or collect food. These are only psychological crutches. They are not needed.

It is rare indeed that a lost person will starve to death or freeze to death if he falls asleep. Downed pilots have spent weeks without a full meal and recovered in fine shape—a little discomfort maybe, but no real problems.

If a fire goes out or you are running out of matches, don't sweat it. It's not that important, even in winter. Curl up under a snowbank or at the base of a tree and go to sleep. Things will look better in the morning.

Don't try walking out of the woods in the dark. The biggest danger will be that you'll poke out an eye on a branch or fall off a cliff. Sit tight.

Keep cool. Sing. Talk to yourself. Remember you are not lost. Everyone else is.

And most of all, forget all the bunk about gathering wood, building a fire or collecting berries and such. Rest. Conserve your energy and think.

The real power is in the mind and your ability to think yourself through difficulties.

—Jerry Chiappetta

THINGS YOU MAY NOT KNOW

Snakes and fish have ears but these ears have no outside openings. They "hear" mostly through vibrations in the ground or water.

The panda has the face of a raccoon, feet like a cat and body similar to that of the bear.

Only the male katydids, crickets and cicadas sing. The females are silent.

Most of the early spring-song of birds is by way of announcing their claim on certain nesting areas.

Gardens in a Jar

With a glass container, some moss, a little dirt and a few well-chosen plants, you can create a rain forest under glass. The terrarium is a wonderful way to introduce your youngster to the wonderful world of gardening.

The miniature greenhouses are fairly simple to put together and easy to care for. It's best to use plants that do not grow rapidly. Any small-leafed ivy, *Peperomia, Fittonia,* small palm, *Philodendron,* fern—these are all ideal for covered container plant growing.

The wide-topped containers are just easier to work with. Bottle neck containers must be carefully maneuvered with long tweezers. Follow these seven steps for a healthy terrarium:

Line the sides of the container with dry moss. This is purely decorative and keeps the gravel from showing through the glass.

Add a layer of gravel or crushed rock for drainage and sprinkle granulated charcoal into the gravel.

Add a moist soil at least one-inch thick.

Arrange plants in the dirt. One veteran terrarium-maker said that she leaves her plants in the peat pots, then covers the pots with the soil. The container retards the growth, which is exactly what you want to do. Almost any plant that grows in a moist, shady spot can adapt to terrarium living.

Water each plant with droplets of water. If you get the plants too moist, they will rot.

Cover the plants to keep them from losing moisture. A cover

of glass should be used (you can improvise one with clear plastic wrap) because you are creating a humid climate for a variety of tropical and semitropical plants.

Place the plants in a north window, turning occasionally to keep the plants growing straight.

If you want to keep a terrarium, you should put it in the most beneficial light. There is absolutely no use in planting one, only to have it fizzle in two weeks. A coffee table in a dark corner is not the proper spot for a terrarium. If you don't have a suitable window, fluorescent lighting is the other alternative.

KEEPING THE KIDS WARM

A simple trick that keeps feet warm in winter involves a common plastic bag found in any kitchen.

Several pairs of medium-weight socks are better than one bulky big pair of socks, but a foot placed inside a plastic bag will really stay warm and dry.

Put on a single pair of medium-weight socks. Now slip the foot into a bag and put on the second pair of socks over the bag.

Place it all inside a bedroom slipper and then into rubber boots and you have an inexpensive and very warm foot gear for severe cold.

If you do much walking in this air-tight setup you can expect to have moist feet which soon become cold feet when you stop walking. Don't outfit the tootsies this way until you arrive at your destination such as your ice fishing spot out on the lake.

—Jerry Chiappetta

HOE! HOE! HOE!

For Sale: "Lawn mower, push-type; used very little, and when used, pushed very, very slowly."

Moderns Go for Pot Plant Gardens

Today, if we asked Mary Contrary how her garden grows, we'd be likely to get a purely twentieth century response. Instead of cockleshells and silver bells, the modern answer is "in containers."

The popularity of pot plant gardens reflects the ease of maintaining them. Selecting flowers and colorful foliage in red clay containers means a weedless garden, one without a need for constant attention. Another asset is instant garden portability. Pot plants are easily moved from porch to patio, from tabletop to terrace floor. And pot gardens allow even the non-gardeners to extend their decorative touches to the outdoors.

Flowering plants in clay pots can be put directly into the ground. Keep the top rim or collar of the pot a little above ground level, so that the soil in the container will not wash away. The porosity of the clay allows moisture and air to reach plant roots when pots are slipped into garden, planter or window box soil.

Even if plants are not "plunged," the thick walls of the clay pot will help protect root structures from overheating, despite exposure to summer temperatures. To further protect plants left on sunny terraces or decks, try double-potting. Simply slip the clay-potted plant into an outer container an inch or two larger than the clay pot. Line the space between the inner and outer pots with sphagnum or peat moss and keep the filler material wet. The plant will draw necessary moisture through its porous pot walls, and the second pot will provide added insulation against summer heat.

Easily portable plantings are a pleasant feature of the pot garden. Flowers grow best in certain sun conditions—geraniums in full sun, fuchsias in shaded areas—but kept in pots, both sun and shade plants can easily be moved to decorate patio or terrace for party occasions. If plants are large and hard to carry, use a plant dolly or wheelbarrow for transporting them.

YOU CAN'T BE TWENTY-NINE FOREVER

I'm over thirty. Have been for several years and have enjoyed every moment of it. Well, there are a few moments I haven't. That's when I hear young people say they never trust anyone over thirty. Let me ask you this: would you trust Socrates, Michelangelo, Cervantes, Verdi, Victor Hugo, Ford or Edison?

I know one fellow you'll be glad didn't hang it up at thirty. Louis Pasteur was in his forties when he saved the French wine industry by inventing the process of "pasteurization." Pasteur was in his sixties when he found the antidote to rabies.

Thomas Alva Edison invented his own personal favorite, the phonograph, at the age of thirty, the electric light at thirty-two and motion pictures at forty. What if he'd packed it in after thirty?

Some of the great writings of all time were written long after their authors had passed that trustable thirty. Charles Dickens was forty-nine when he finished *Great Expectations.* Victor Hugo wrote *Les Miserables* at sixty. Shakespeare wrote *Hamlet* when thirty-seven and *The Tempest* was in his forty-eighth year. Cervantes started *Don Quixote* in his fifties and finished it long after most people retire.

While we are enthralled with stores of "child prodigy" musicians, Handel was fifty-seven when he finished the *Messiah.* Bach wrote some of his finest masses in his late forties and fifties. Beethoven's last quartet works in his fifties are considered among his finest. Verdi's *Otello* was a product of his seventies.

Isaac Newton formulated his principles of gravity in his early twenties, but didn't finalize them on paper until twenty years later. Albert Einstein's theory of relativity was first propounded when he was thirty-one and became generally accepted ten years later.

Henry Ford was forty before he founded his motor car company. Orville Wright was thirty-two and Wilbur Wright was thirty-six when they got their plane off the ground. Incidentally, both took place seventy years ago in 1903.

Michelangelo began the Sistine Chapel ceiling at fifty-eight and finished it when he was sixty-six. Leonardo da Vinci did the world's most famous painting, Mona Lisa, when he was in his mid-fifties.

I think you get the point. There is no point in time when people quit producing and become useless. Plants are like this, too. While it is always more exciting, more challenging to try something new in your yard and garden, it is the wise gardener who knows when to pay some attention to his old friends. I know this much—I never met a tree over thirty years old that I didn't like.

THINGS YOU MAY NOT KNOW

Raccoon gets its name from the fact that it washes its food before eating it. The name raccoon is a derivation of the Indian name arathcone, *meaning "the washer."*

A transparent membrane protects flying birds' eyes from dust, twigs and other hazards.

Fish and porcupine are among the favorite foods of the fisher. Legend says his name comes from stealing fish used to bait marten traps.

The bobcat, like many nocturnal creatures, has eyes that adjust admirably to extreme light conditions. The pupil is small and elliptical in bright light, large and round in dim light.

Any Room Can Be a Garden Room

There's no need to start from architectural scratch to achieve the popular garden look. Almost any room in the house can qualify. A garden room can be anything from a specially built sun porch to a converted garage, from family to laundry room, or dining area.

The most important ingredients of the garden look are living plants and flowers, healthfully and naturally displayed in porous, red clay containers. It also includes color schemes which stress the outdoor tones of green, blue, and yellow, as well as good amounts of white. Floral prints in fabrics, wallpapers, curtains and carpets are important, too. And so is casual furniture—made of wicker and rattan—no longer restricted to outdoor areas.

The potted plant collections, which set the mood for garden areas, must always be in top shape. To assure your plants a healthy beginning, select them from local florists and garden stores who condition and sell their plants in porous, red clay pots. Unglazed, thick-walled clay containers allow oxygen to enter through porous walls to strengthen the root systems of plants. Clay pots also slowly leach out excess water which otherwise would clog roots and cause plant failure.

When selecting plants for your indoor garden choose those plants suitable to the light conditions available. If your indoor garden area is a sunless dining room or a windowless laundry area, you'll have to make your plant selections carefully.

Though all plants need light, some foliage types do well in shaded areas. These plants include Chinese evergreens, *Schefflera,* jade plants, rubber plants and *Philodendron.* These greens differ in size, shape, and richness of foliage, so a varied and interesting pot garden can be achieved with "dim" prospects. Of course, artificial light may be substituted for natural growing conditions. Many home gardeners maintain elaborate collections under fluorescent lighting.

Another hazard to the indoor garden is hot, dry air. To increase atmospheric humidity in a garden area, try grouping plants in a pebble garden. Cluster the plants on pebble-lined trays, with the pebble layer kept constantly moist. The resulting evaporation will keep the air around the plants humid.

To vary the effect of a totally green garden, it's an excellent idea to mix seasonal flowering plants among the foliage. Some flowering plants such as the chrysanthemum, African violet, gloxinia, and azalea are available all year long, while others such as the geranium and tuberous begonia are strictly seasonal. Many of the flowering pot plants can be planted outdoors after their indoor blooming period is finished.

GRASSHOPPERS ARE FOR DRINKING, TOO

I've often wondered why mint is the only thing from the yard that legitimately finds its way into mixed drinks? Mint juleps are internationally famous.

But I think things may be changing. The bartender is going through a growing stage and I look for him to turn to the flower beds and shrubs to help dress up his drinks.

I've already seen evidence of this in some of the polynesian restaurants now offering orchids floating in certain exotic drinks. Most of these look a lot better than they taste.

But you can discover some fragrant and refreshing herbs that will enhance your drinks.

The hottest new drink in years was a Harvey Wallbanger, which the nation's airline stewardesses help popularize. It's made of Galliano, vodka and orange juice.

While the following may have different names in different sections of the country, here are a few of the delightful new names for mixed drinks (and their contents) which may help your garden *glow:*

Rob Roy: sweet vermouth, Scotch, orange bitters and lemon peel.

Silver Bullet: gin, vermouth, Scotch.

Greek Martini: vodka, mavrodaphne, lemon juice, lemon peel.

Bull Shot: vodka, Worcestershire sauce, beef bouillon, lime.

Grasshopper: green crème de menthe, light crème de cacao, cream.

Velvet Hammer: light crème de cacao, Cointreau, cream.

Pink Squirrel: crème de noyau, crème de cacao, cream.

Golden Dream: Galliano, Cointreau, orange juice, cream.

Golden Cadillac: Galliano, light crème de cacao, cream.

HOE! HOE! HOE!

Many a determined wife has turned an old rake into a lawn mower.

Our forefathers could run a farm with less machinery than we require to keep a lawn today.

New homeowner plants a lawn and hopes the plot thickens.

When grass looks greener on the other side of the fence remember it could mean they just know a better brand of fertilizer.

Plants Are Top Decorators' Darlings

Next time you walk through the model rooms in your favorite furniture or department store, take a look at the increasing numbers of living plants used by top decorators to glamorize the settings. They'll range from such small plants as ferns to large tree-like varieties like palms or *Dracaena*—the decorators' darlings.

Their popularity is really not much of a mystery. These plants may vary in size, but they all have one quality in common. Their foliage is individualized. They have a "sculptured" look that appeals to the professional eye.

Let's take the large plants first. The palm family includes some outstanding house plants with a wonderfully feathery, yet durable, leaf. From Phoenix to Kenya, palms enhance their surroundings. They're especially appropriate with the new garden look, as well as with oriental accents. Most palms need light, but no direct sunlight. They thrive in semi-shady to shady quarters in average house temperatures, with their soil kept evenly moist, so porous clay containers are a must for proper drainage.

The *Dracaena* most often used as a large, decorative, showpiece plant is called *Dracaena gracilis*. With its linear leaves that spread out and upward from a single, thin, bark-like stem, this *Dracaena* perfectly coordinates with contemporary furniture.

The plant itself is almost an angular piece of sculpture. They need adequate light and the good, natural drainage provided by clay pots.

Ferns are the least in size, but perhaps the most versatile decoratively. The Boston fern with its flowing fronds is a special favorite. A flourishing fern plant is a bouquet of greenery, which, on closer inspection, proves to be a gracefully arching collection of individual fronds made up of small, delicate leaves. The plant mixes well with any style in furnishings; small enough to blend with fragile antique pieces and full enough to combine with the hearty Spanish look. Ferns need good moisture, humidity and light. An excellent way to use them is to set their clay pots on a pebble-covered tray, water the pebble layer, and let the plants absorb needed humidity through resulting evaporation. It also creates an attractive garden-like effect indoors.

TIPS AND TRICKS

Rub the male ferrule of your jointed fishing rod along your nose or through your hair to keep it from sticking. Rubbing it with the lead of a pencil will also work well. It is the graphite that helps.

Plastic worms are becoming very popular with anglers, but they wilt in very hot weather. Keep them in a small jar of water. It won't bother the plastic worms. They'll last indefinitely.

Nightcrawlers in a can of earth always dig to the bottom of the container. It's a bother when you want one for fishing so cut both ends off a clean can and use plastic snap-on lids. Simply turn it over each time you need a fresh worm. He'll be there right handy.

Try a furniture polish of three parts olive oil, one part vinegar (like the base for French dressing).

Remove rust from utensils with a cork dipped in olive oil.

Clean white fur or fake fur by rubbing it with dry cornmeal.

Break up old cigarette butts and save used pipe tobacco. Place them in open containers in your closets and the moths will stay away.

Dieters, instead of using oil or butter to fry fish, cook them in grapefruit juice for a taste that's terrific.

To clean eyeglasses without streaks use a drop of vinegar on each lens, or a drop of gin or vodka.

Colorful ice in a punch bowl: Fill a clean balloon with tinted water and freeze. Peel off the balloon and the ice ball will be ready to use.

Coffee and clothes: When a lot of coffee is left over, freeze into cubes and use to add to the rinse water for dark colored clothes. For some reason this prevents lint from sticking.

THINGS YOU MAY NOT KNOW

Crickets' chirps have surprising carrying power. One cricket barely an inch long sounds a note audible for almost a mile.

It is safe to hold a queen bee in your hand as the queen bees use their stingers only on other queen bees.

Young flounders start life quite normally, with one eye on each side of the head. But as they begin to swim and rest on one side, one eye begins to migrate until both are on the upper side of the head.

Natural Room Accessories

Add fresh touches to your home this fall with living plants, thoughtfully selected, imaginatively placed and properly cared for.

Plants are the natural accessory—but don't select them at random. There are certain varieties that look best with specific furniture styles.

For contemporary furniture, a grouping of the large tropical green plants, such as *Schefflera* and *Philodendron,* are excellent choices. They soften the lines of modern, rectangular furniture and the box-like shape of today's rooms. Also appropriate in this type of setting are the more stylized of the foliage plants—*Dracaena* and palms. Although large in size, their foliage is spiked and individualized and they can stand singly, serving as living sculpture.

Large-leafed foliage plants also look well with the Mediterranean styles, so popular now. Ferns and unpretentious mums in their natural clay pots are perfect for this furniture, too.

With traditional, more formal furniture, use smaller plants to complement the more delicate scale of the pieces. Flowering plants, ferns and the flowing varieties of foliage, such as ivy, are good.

Plants generally look most attractive where they are important to design function: a long, narrow entranceway having as its dramatic focus a tall palm; a massing of different sizes of fairly substantial foliage plants combined with wall shelves that overflow with greenery transforms a modest dining area into an indoor garden nook; a monochrome color scheme can be brought to life with red clay pots of golden and russet-colored chrysanthemums.

There are innumerable ways to use living plants decoratively, but the most imaginative touches will be ruined by ill-kept plants. So, know a few of the basics of plant care.

Select quality plants from reputable florists and garden centers.

Well-grown plants will be locally conditioned and sold in porous clay pots. Used by top professional growers, the unglazed clay pots protect against overwatering—the major cause of house plant failure.

When you buy plants, find out their needs. Check on watering, light and temperature requirements. With a bit of effort, plant selections will thrive and remain decorative bonuses.

WHAT'S IN A NAME?

When you gals get ready to write your big confessional novel, don't worry about names for your characters. This handy little guide from a confessions magazine editor will help you decide:

Will, Tom, Jerry and Stan: Hard workers whom girls should marry; usually work in physical-type jobs.

Rod, Rhett, Roscoe, Rupert and Raymond: Bad guys, with whom girls have affairs, but never marry.

Rita and Maria: Fast women, with whom the Wills and Toms think of having affairs.

Madge: She lives next door, sharing her coffee pot and shoulder with long-suffering wives and sweethearts.

Roger and Ralph: Usually creeps who get crushes on the heroine.

Norman: Always the momma's boy.

Greg: Best-looking fellow, who moans when he kisses.

Johnny: Bad guy who turns out all right in the end.

Betty: Sister-in-law, who keeps a spotless house and whose children are well-behaved.

Derek and Nick: Fast workers, very rich and very smart.

Alice, Ann, and Amy: You.

Pesticides and the Environment

Much has been said in recent years of the effects of pesticides in our environment. Critics often feel that little or nothing is known about what happens to a pesticide once it is applied. They do not realize that pesticide residues are being monitored in human body fat, in the nation's rivers, lakes and estuaries, in air, in soil and in many species of wildlife.

These monitoring studies show it is not true that all pesticides have had a similar impact on the environment and human health, resulting in each case in an environmental buildup. In

Lake Michigan, for example, while residues of DDT have been found, no residues of chlordane or heptachlor have been found.

A quick summary regarding the information known about chlordane illustrates the depth of knowledge concerning pesticides. Chlordane is used for control of insects in and around the home, in lawns and gardens, on golf courses, and in agriculture. There have been extensive studies, both in the laboratory and under actual use conditions, of chlordane and its effect on the environment and human health.

Chlordane is primarily a soil insecticide; therefore, any consideration of possible environmental effect must place significant emphasis on the fate of chlordane in the soil. It is immobile in the soil, does not leach and therefore does not move within the environment to any significant degree. Studies show that soil applications of chlordane do not result in residue buildup and also that residues do not increase with repetitive annual applications. When one to two pounds of chlordane per acre are applied, 50 percent remains after one year, 5 percent remains after four years, and after six years, only one percent remains.

Surveys by the U.S. Department of Interior show that chlordane does not contaminate ground or surface waters. In 1967, for example, only one out of 223 samples showed a trace of chlordane and that was 0.0036 ppm, an insignificant amount. It was not detected in any waters sampled in 1968.

Feeding studies have shown that ingestion of chlordane results in its metabolism to hydrophilic metabolites and only a minute and insignificant portion is stored in fatty tissues. Workers under medical observation employed in the manufacturing of chlordane have shown no evidence of adverse effects on their health and well-being. Similarly, there is no evidence of adverse effect on workers formulating or applying chlordane.

Food and Drug Administration surveys between 1966 and 1968 show that the dietary intake of chlordane is either undetectable or too low to quantitate. Only one trace of chlordane was measured during one year, and this amount was insignificant and negligible. In summary, both experience and experiment support the conclusion that chlordane, as currently allowed to be used, is safe.

A problem for the chemical industry is the current tendency of publicity and casual comment to categorize pesticides into classes, such as chlorinated hydrocarbons or phosphates, as though each pesticide in each group were one and the same. This has led to many misconceptions. Heptachlor, chlordane, DDT and endrin, for example, are all classified as chlorinated hydrocarbons, but they are applied in different ways, control different insects, sell for widely different prices, and have widely ranging toxicities and other properties.

Each chemical—whether long used or newly developed—must be considered on its own merit and in terms of each prescribed use. Across-the-board bans of specific chemicals or classifications of chemicals are not an appropriate answer to our need for effective insect control.

What has engendered many problems is the fact that the chemicals in the chlorinated hydrocarbon class can be detected by exquisitely sensitive methods. The gas chromatograph, for example, picks up the chlorinated hydrocarbons down to one part per billion and even one part per trillion—levels where few other compounds can be detected. Unfortunately, many persons would rather conclude that any level whatever is harmful, rather than consider what effects the presence of a compound at one part per billion or one part per trillion has on the environment.

What is needed in the dialogue concerning pesticides and the environment is less rhetoric and more reason. Critics of the chemical industry seem willing to substitute materials we know little about—microorganisms, for example—for chemicals that have been used successfully for years with marginal, if any, damage to the environment.

Most laymen who have proposed the use of hormones, predators and microorganisms for insect control fail to recognize that such agents are potentially hazardous. Predators, for example, can turn out to be worse pests than the insects they are meant to control. Microorganisms, under certain conditions, can reproduce so rapidly and in such great numbers that they become epidemic. Moreover, microorganisms can be more persistent than any of the insecticides developed since the 1940s.

The solution is neither simple nor readily at hand. Although it is reasonable to consider limiting certain uses of certain pesticides when scientific evidence supports the need for such action, we must continue to meet the objectives of controlling damaging insects without harm to human health and the environment.

DO TIMES REALLY CHANGE?

Three timely observations:

1. "Our earth is degenerate in these latter days. Bribery and corruption are common. Children no longer obey their parents. Every man wants to write a book. The end of the world is evidently approaching."

2. "It is a gloomy moment in history. Not for many years has there been so much apprehension. Never has the future seemed so incalculable. . . . Of our own troubles in the United States, no man can see the end."

3. "We live in an unhappy age. . . . No century, perhaps, is more characterized by unhappiness than this."

The first was carved on a stone slab in Assyria in 2800 B.C. The second appeared in *Harper's Weekly* on October 10, 1857. And the third comes from a magazine, the *New Englander* of January, 1879. Does *tempus* really *fugit?*

At today's prices, no one can meat the budget.

Organic or Chemical Gardening?

I would have to say that more people are more confused about organic and chemical gardening than any two gardening subjects you could name. The sprayers and anti-sprayers lock horns constantly and ask me to arbitrate. I tell them that the truth is somewhere between them and they find this stance hard to believe. Forget the fads and what's fashionable. Let's look at facts.

Our minds have been exposed to the evils of pesticides to the world population—people, plants, and animals included. And it's well that we have been made aware of the problem. Several of our chemicals did leave harmful residues and have deservedly been relegated to the waste dump. But how about the hundreds of other chemicals that do their jobs and break down quickly leaving no toxic residues? Unfortunately, these chemicals are catching a bad case of overflow antagonism.

Let's take a look at some research work conducted by Dr. Robert Lambe, plant pathologist with Virginia Polytechnic Institute. Lambe was interested in determining the merits and demerits of chemical and organic gardening. Identical plots were used and the same varieties grown in each. In fact, all conditions were carefully kept identical, except that one of the plots was fertilized chemically and sprayed as necessary, while manures and organic pest control measures were used on the other.

Soil in each plot was found by soil test to be relatively

infertile. The organic garden received a thousand pounds of dehydrated cow manure, a good soil conditioner, but a diluted fertilizer. The chemically protected garden was treated with a hundred pounds of 10-10-10. Both gardens then received the same amount of actual nitrogen, phosphorous and potassium, and both fertilizers were worked into the soil. Cost for the organic plot was $50, compared to $3.15 for the chemically protected garden.

Weeds were kept under control in each garden. A soil "sterilizing" chemical was used on the chemically treated plot before planting (cost, $37.08).

The organic garden was hand weeded (nine hours at $2 per hour; cost, $18). Amounts and frequency of irrigation were identical.

The important figure to look at is the total cost per pound. Results of Lambe's experiment show that vegetables grown organically could cost the grower 59 cents per pound; those chemically produced could cost 8 cents per pound. From 59 cents the vegetables would have to be marked up at least twice more for the wholesalers' and the grocers' profits. That might mean that a head of cabbage would sell for $1.50 and a big juicy tomato for 80 cents.

Contrary to occasional opinions, you can't taste the difference between chemically treated and organically grown fruits and vegetables. Moreover, organically grown vegetables are probably no more wholesome for your family.

Any plant physiologist in the world can tell you that nitrogen is nitrogen, and potash is potash, when they enter the plant. It makes absolutely no difference whether the elements have come from rotted manure or right out of the chemical factory. They must break down to exactly the same material before they enter the plant's roots.

Thus, the case for the totally "organic" garden doesn't seem so strong. The wise and successful gardener needs to take the middle-of-the-road approach. Study all the facts.

OLD WIVES AND THEIR TALES

I wish I had a penny for every time I've had to listen to someone ask me or tell me about horticultural old wives' tales. The worst thing about these tales is that they are always emphatically told as the gospel, according to that elusive and know-it-all authority known as, "They Say."

The "They-Sayers" sure have gotten this world fouled up and in a foul mood, too. But, let's take a look at some of the frequently asked questions, which deal in some degree with the tales of the old wives.

I know when I get into apple-growing country someone will tell me: "Apple trees are naturally resistant to insect and disease pests." I know of no place in the United States where a reasonably profitable crop of apples can be grown year after year without the use of protective devices against insect and disease pests. To this end, I've known many home gardeners who have become convinced it is easier to buy their fruit than grow it.

People use these old wives' tales as excuses for not doing something. Too often I hear people say they don't want to mess with roses because they require so much "special care" to protect them against pests. This is pure nonsense. Roses don't require that much kid-gloving. Usually, one of the all-purpose pesticides (applied in either liquid spray or dust form) will do the trick to keep your roses free of pests and diseases.

Lots of garden fanciers will swear that garden seeds stored more than a year are useless. These people, I suspect, have stock in seed firms. The longevity of many seeds depends, for the most part, on the conditions under which the seed was grown and how it has been stored. Keeping seeds in stoppered bottles in a cool basement helps them live for at least two seasons.

Now when it comes to tulip bulbs, new bulbs are preferred to those saved from last year. These spring-bloomers have bulbs that can make it for only one season. Replant with new bulbs each year.

Old wives will probably tell you to prune all brown leaves

from broad-leafed evergreens in early spring. Why be in such a rush? Those leaves may be brown, but check the twigs closely. They still may be green.

How to water your lawn and garden is knee-deep in old wives' tales. Some advocate sprinkling, some say flood. I say they're all wet. A good soaking is better than several sprinklings and certainly better than flooding, which is really a drowning. Light sprinklings, as a matter of fact, can be quite harmful. A little water applied to the surface of the soil may bring out young rootlets. It is far better to moisten the soil fully, feeding the deeper roots in their natural growth.

"All I need is good, rich soil and I can grow a great lawn without putting anything on it." I've heard this tale from an old husband. I always tell such braggarts: we'll take identical soils, you plant without fertilizers, and I'll plant with 'em. I can guarantee that my yard will be greater. Fertilization is not a dirty word.

I think maybe if we could get some of these old and new wives off their tails and out in the yards and gardens working, they wouldn't have to spread these tales. And a little exercise will prevent those other tails from spreading, too.

THINGS YOU MAY NOT KNOW

Except for vultures and parrots, Canada geese live longer than any other birds. Authentic records of birds in captivity give them as much as seventy years.

The hippopotamus differs from the rhinoceros in having four instead of three toes.

The newly born kangaroo is only about an inch long and is semi-transparent as an earthworm.

The courting dance of the Prince Rudolph Bird of Paradise is performed upside-down on a branch.

Vampire bats, when on the ground, are said to be able to run as fast as a rat.

Plants Have Feelings

How many times have you heard the saying, "we must communicate with nature," and passed it off as a whimsical quip by some nature nut? If we are going to improve our ecological situation and find a solution to pollution then we must change our attitudes and heed the advice of the so-called nature nut and seriously practice this old saying.

How do you communicate with nature? The same way you communicate with a person or a pet—use patience and kindness. Plants react to conditions and situations in exactly the same way that you and I do.

Cleve Backster, a noted and respected polygraph expert, has been experimenting for several years with plants and their emotions. He has written many articles on the subject, and has appeared on most of the television talk shows demonstrating the results. Backster has proved that plants experience pleasurable emotions when they're fed, watered or pampered. These emotions are recorded on the lie detector. In other tests, he writes that when plants are exposed to physical danger, such as burning or cutting, they show the symptoms of pure animal fear. In a recent test run by Baxter, using several of his students, it was concluded that plants can possibly indicate who committed a crime. One of the students was secretly assigned to assassinate one of two plants in the laboratory during the night by mutilating it. The next day the polygraph was attached to the surviving plant. Each student was then brought into the room, one at a time. When the assassin's turn came, the poly-graph's needle jumped all over the paper.

Cleve Backster is not the only one conducting this type of experiment. Most of the major pharmaceutical and chemical companies are also studying the parallels between plants and people.

I have said many times that plants love music and grow better when exposed to the sound waves of the latest hits. Other researchers agree with me. We only disagree on the type of music they like. In one recent report I saw, it said that after plants were exposed to three hours of rock and roll music they simply withered and died. Yet the plants in my home are exposed to the most violent collection of rock tunes available for periods much longer than three hours, day in and day out, with no adverse effects whatsoever. On the contrary, I have trouble confining their growing performance. To clarify the overabundance of rock sounds in our home, I need only remind you that we have three teen-age daughters. I will conclude this music phase of our nature communications course by saying that our house plants do seem to relax a little better in the evening when my wife and I listen to Mantovani.

Screaming and bickering households are not, as a rule, ideal surroundings for growing plants. I must define screaming and bickering as opposed to the yelling and hollering of children. Plants prefer a stable pattern of noise, rather than constant surprises like "Boo!" and jumping through a doorway. Vicious and vindictive quarreling will turn almost all plants into neu-rotic introverts. The reason for this is your care of the plants when you are under a mental strain will be reflected in your physical handling of the plant itself, resulting many times in fatal damage to the plant. Do not, under any circumstances touch or feed, cultivate or otherwise tend to your garden or plants when you are emotionally upset. You will more than likely hurt them without really meaning to when in this state. Just talk, don't touch.

Plants are possessive and tend to become jealous when some one or something alienates the affections of their master. Thi can be a new baby, puppy, husband or wife. But in most cases, it is the result of a new plant which is brought into the home and receives more attention than the older plant. When jealousy is the problem, the new growth stops, flowers cease, but the plant does not die nor get sick. It just simply pouts. This can be overcome by setting up a schedule before the arrival of any of the above listed. It is important that you do not neglect the plants and, whenever possible, give them an extra turn each day. You can't kill a plant with this type of kindness.

Verbal communication with plants is possible and has been recommended for hundreds of years—tell it to a rose, talk to the trees, and so forth. I talk to myself most of the time so my associates do not think too much of it when I wander around the greenhouse discussing the day's events with my potted friends. Potted plants, that is.

Thousands of people have come up to me and confessed that they must be a little nuts because they talk to their plants. I tell them they aren't alone, that the real nuts are the people who don't talk to their plants.

GEOGRAPHY BETWEEN BREAD

I guess I spend as much time "eating on the run" as anyone I know. Between coast to coast trips to appear on television shows, I also find myself all over the country on lecture or promotional tours.

I can almost tell where I am by what type of sandwich I'm served "on the run" and by what the sandwich is called. People who dig the outdoors are usually sandwich freaks, too.

Sandwiches take up so little room in a backpack and are just the thing with a glass of milk or tea when you're pruning or planting and are too dirty or sweaty to sit down at the table.

We all owe our delight in the sandwich to a compulsive gambler, the Earl of Sandwich, who had a chef invent the "sandwich"—two pieces of bread to hold a hot piece of meat— so the Earl wouldn't have to leave the card table.

Wonder what would have happened if he'd been the Earl of Canterbury? "Say, what would you like on your canterbury, buddy?"

Nope, it's best he was from Sandwich.

But you can know where most folks are from by what they call one of those sandwiches on which everything is placed. If you're in Baltimore, Detroit or Los Angeles it's a Submarine.

In Philadelphia, Washington and Des Moines it's called a Hoagie.

You'll find yourself ordering a Poor Boy in Houston, Sacramento and Montgomery, but a Po' Boy in New Orleans and Memphis.

San Francisco natives eat Grinders, just like the folks in Toledo, Cleveland and Providence.

In Reno and Gary, Indiana, it's a Torpedo. You get an Italian Sandwich in Louisville and Reading.

Miamians buy Cuban Sandwiches, while Buffalo snackers get a Bomber with their beer.

Cincinnati's beer fanciers chase their Rockets with the brew.

New Yorkers, naturally, call their big sandwiches the Hero.

By far, the biggest name for the biggest sandwich is the Submarine, derived from the sub-shaped bread—usually a long loaf of French bread. The Hoagie, many feel, came from Hogans, the name once applied to Irish laborers who ate meat-stuffed long rolls.

I have traced the history of these sandwiches in many cities and discovered they all seem to have originated in each city's bread basket.

The New Orleans Po' Boy originated in a French Market cafe around 1921. Nuns in New Orleans copied this sandwich, passing out these stuffed loaves when waifs and street urchins came around convents begging for a *pourboire,* or handout.

New Orleans probably has the greatest Po' Boy sandwich in the world, but be sure you order the sandwich with the "debris" intact—that's the bread and meat crumbs that are created by the slice. New Orleans sandwich-makers place this debris inside the sandwich, making it a very special taste, or at least that's the sales pitch they give you way down yonder in New Orleans.

I have found that sandwich shops flourish in and around most farmer's markets, where working people like the rib-sticking quality of sandwiches stuffed with meats and cheeses and various garden produce.

If we had to choose the all-American sandwich, it would be the hamburger hands-down, or hands-around. But even the hamburger gives away its geographic location.

For example, Boston hamburgers often are served with a baked-bean topping.

San Francisco burgers are served on sourdough rolls.

Most Texas burgers have liberal toppings of chili.

In southern cities hamburgers are served with cole slaw.

California hamburgers are served with everything.

Detroit has one of the most unusual hamburgers—the Coney Island hamburger—which is loose-fried, spicy hamburger meat, topped with mustard, onions and chili.

American sandwiches and hamburgers also have international influence. A layer-on-top-of-layer sandwich in Europe is known as the Dagwood after the famous comic character's midnight-snack creations. And all over London and Paris you will see Wimpy stands, serving up hamburgers made internationally famous by Popeye's fat friend.

The sandwich is as much a part of the American life-style as the flower bed and lawn mowing.

governor is attached to each state to make it go slower.

oil erosion is the Great Terrain Robbery.

yawn is the world's only honest opinion.

rain is when the air has more moisture than it knows what to dew with.

Time Saving Chart

To make sure you do not waste your time, effort and money, here is a list of annuals and their uses for your quick references:

FOR BORDERS

Ageratum	Petunia	Cynoglossum
Alyssum	Salvia farinacea and	Larkspur
Balsam	splendens	Snapdragon
Bells of Ireland	Centaurea	Statice
Marigold	Cleome	Zinnia
Nicotiana	Cosmos	

FOR COLOR

Amaranthus	Coleus	Kochia
Basil	Dusty Miller	Perilla
Canna		

FOR PARTIAL SHADE

Balsam	Coleus	Nicotiana
Begonia	Impatiens	Pansy
Browallia	Lobelia	Salvia
Calendula	Myosotis	Torenia

FOR THE SEASIDE

Alyssum	Hollyhock	Petunia
Dusty Miller	Lupine	Statice

FOR WINDOW BOXES

Alyssum	Coleus	Cascade Petunias
Begonia	Lobelia	Thunbergia
semperflorens	Nierembergia	

TALL GROWERS

Amaranthus	Cleome	Marigold
Aster	Cosmos	Scabiosa
Celosia (Tall *Plumosa*	Dahlia (such as	Statice
sorts such as	Cactus and Giant	Snapdragon
Forest Fire)	Flowered types)	(Rockets)
Centaurea (Bachelor	Hollyhock	Zinnia
Buttons)	Larkspur	

GROUND COVERS

Cobaea
Creeping Zinnia
   (Sanvitalia
   Procumbens)
Lobelia
Mesembryanthemum

Morning Glory
Mysostis
Nasturtium
Nierembergia
Portulaca

Sweet Alyssum
Sweet Pea
Thunbergia
Verbena
Vinca

IN THE ROCK GARDEN

Alyssum
Dusty Miller
Candytuft

Gazania
Mesembryanthemum
Pansy

Verbena
Plus ground
   covers

FOR EDGING

Ageratum
Alyssum
Begonia
Calendula
Candytuft
Centaurea (Dwarf
   Bachelor Buttons)
Celosia (Dwarf such
   as Fiery Feather or
   Jewel Box)
Coleus
Dianthus

Dusty Miller (such
   as *Centaurea Can-*
   dissima and
   Cineraria Maritima
   Diamond)
Gazania
Gomphrena
Heliotrope
Impatiens
Lobelia
Mesembryanthemum
Mysostis

Nierembergia
Phlox
Pansy
Petunia
Portulaca
Snapdragon
   (Floral Carpet)
Torenia
Verbena
Vinca
Zinnia-dwarf

FOR CUTTING

Asters
Bells of Ireland
Carnation
Celosia
Centaurea (Bachelor
   Buttons)
Cosmos
Cynoglossum
Dahlia

Daisy, Tahoka
Gaillardia
Gerbera
Gomphrena
Larkspur
Marigold
Nasturtium
Petunia

Rudbeckia
Salpiglossis
Salvia
Scabiosa
Snapdragon
Statice
Verbena
Zinnia

MEDIUM GROWERS (12 to 24 inches)

Balsam
Basil
Bells of Ireland
Carnation
Celosia (medium
   cristata types such
   as Fireglow)
Cynoglossum
Dahlia (such as
   Unwin's dwarf mix)

Dusty Miller
   (*Centaurea*
   Gymnocarpa)
Gaillardia
Gomphrena
Helichrysum
Impatiens
Nicotiana
Petunia
Rudbeckia

Salpiglossis
Salvia
Snapdragon
   (Vacationland,
   Hit Parade,
   Sprites, Knee
   High)
Verbena
Zinnia

My Handy List of Government-Approved Plant "Medications"

The U.S. Environmental Protection Agency or your local State Department of Agriculture today approves all spray materials sold in garden centers and hardware stores. Most sprays are relatively short-lived: all are safe for use in the home garden when used as directed. If you have questions regarding use and application in your area, consult your store, university extension service, or a garden club.

The following is a list of common yard and garden problem and the spray materials often recommended by gardening experts to control them. Many of these insecticides and fungicide are mixed and available in standard formulations to give mor general control of pests.

PEST	WHAT TO USE	SUGGESTIONS
Ants	Chlordane, Diazinon	Apply when present. Try to locate and treat nest

Aphids	Diazinon, Malathion, Nicotine Sulphate, Pyrethrum, Rotenone	Spray foliage thoroughly with force. Repeat as needed.
Beetles	Carbaryl (Sevin), Diazinon, Malathion	Recommend wettable powder formulations on fruits and vegetables.
Borers	Carbaryl, Lindane	Care and timing important to kill eggs in egg-laying period.
Caterpillars	Carbaryl, Diazinon, Malathion, Oil Spray, Rotenone	Short residual life. Use oil spray in water in very early spring for over-wintering eggs.
Chinch Bugs and Sod Webworms	Aspon, Carbaryl, Diazinon, Malathion, Trithion	Spray lawns when bugs first become present. Water well into thatch. Spray lawn edges thoroughly.
Cutworms	Carbaryl, Diazinon	Do not spray Diazinon on foliage.
Grasshoppers	Carbaryl, Diazinon, Malathion	Spray foliage when grasshoppers are present.
Gypsy Moths	Carbaryl, Methoxychlor	Carbaryl has residual life for about five days. Spray tree crowns well.
Japanese Beetles	Carbaryl, Malathion	Apply as necessary.
Leafhoppers	Carbaryl, Diazinon, Malathion, Pyrethrum	Leafhoppers carry many plant viruses: early summer sprays important.
Leafminers	Diazinon, Malathion, Meta Systox-R	Spray foliage thoroughly when mines appear. Repeat in 10-12 days.

Mites (Red Spiders)	Diazinon, Dicofol (Kelthane), Malathion, Oil Spray	Be sure to treat underside of leaves. Apply 2-3 times at weekly intervals. Apply oil spray in early spring.
Fleas, Ticks	Carbaryl, Diazinon	Spray cracks and crevices.
Mosquitoes	Malathion, Pyrethrum	Also eliminate all standing water that mosquitoes use as breeding grounds. Spray underneath leaves, foundations, under porches where mosquitoes rest.
Snails, Slugs	Metaldehyde	Spray infested areas especially near borders and lawn edges. Control is slow but sure.
Scale Insects	Carbaryl, Diazinon, Malathion, Oil Spray	Spray in "crawler" stage, usually late spring; certain soft scale species hatch in late summer, early fall. Apply dormant sprays before new growth appears; repeat spraying may be necessary.
Tarnished Plant Bugs	Carbaryl, Diazinon, Malathion	Best control achieved when bugs are small (nymph stage).
Tent Caterpillar	Carbaryl, Diazinon, Malathion	Spray when nests are first noticed. Care must be taken to spray tree thoroughly.

Termites	Chlordane	For best control, long residual life is required in soil and under buildings.
Thrips	Carbaryl, Diazinon, Malathion, Rotenone	Tiny insects; often feed inside buds and scar foliage. Weekly spraying may be needed.
Worms (Bag, Web and Canker)	Carbaryl, Diazinon, Dormant Oils, Malathion	Apply oil spray for dormant eggs. Bagworms best controlled in early summer.
Black Spot	Benlate, Maneb (Fore or Dithane M-22 Special or Dithane M-45), Folpet	Thorough coverage of all plant surfaces necessary.
Chickweed, Knotweed, Clover	Dicamba, MCPP, 2, 4, 5-TP (Silvex)	Repeat applications may be necessary. Be careful on sensitive southern grasses.
Crabgrass	Ammonium Methyl Arsonate	For post-emergence. Use with care. Even application important.
Dandelions, Plantain	2,4-D	Care needed when using volatile esters. Use one-half rate on some southern grasses.
Powdery Mildew	Acti-Dione PM, Dinocap (Karathane)	Thorough coverage of all plant surfaces necessary.

MY BAKER'S DOZEN OF SPRAYING COMMANDMENTS

1. Select the right sprayer for the job. Buy the best quality you can afford. It will make spraying easier and, with good care, your sprayer will last for years. And be sure to get one that gives you full control of spray mix and application!

2. Before you spray, be sure to read *all* of the sprayer directions—right down to the warranty. "Test drive" your new sprayer using water to see how it works and what it will do.

3. Mix your spray materials *exactly* according to instructions.

4. Choose the right pressure. Use a high pressure for a fine, penetrating mist (good for flowers). Use lower pressure if you want a heavier, wetting, non-drift spray (best for weeds).

5. *Spot* spray, don't broadcast. Spray only to the point of run-off. Avoid drenching. And waste.

6. Spray where the trouble is. Because most trouble starts *under* the plant leaves, it is especially important that you spray there. Cover the entire stem system too. Spraying on target avoids waste in time and material.

7. Use an adjustable nozzle to produce a fine cone-shaped mist for close-up applications and a coarser spray for long-range spraying or for weeds.

8. For maximum effectiveness—not to mention less wear and tear on you—spray in the cool of the day.

9. To prevent drifting of spray to non-target areas, don't spray when the wind is blowing.

10. If you prefer to dust plants, apply the dust in the morning or evening when the air is still and when dew on the plants makes the dust stick better.

11. Dress sensibly. Don't wear shorts or a bathing suit. It's a

good idea to wear gloves (plastic throw-aways will do) and a hat if you're spraying above your head or at eye level. Wear shoes. I recommend that you wear your golf spikes when working in the yard. The spikes do two jobs at once: improve your traction on uneven ground, and aerate the lawn.

12. Thoroughly drain and clean your sprayer when finished. Use a mild solution of warm soap and water. Wipe your equipment dry when finished. (It upsets me to go into a garden shed and find dirty equipment). Good care will make your equipment last for many, many seasons, making it an even better investment.

13. Store sprays and dusts out of reach of children, preferably in a locked cabinet. Keep sprays in original containers. Be sure labels are kept on containers. Do not burn empty containers.

THINGS YOU MAY NOT KNOW

The bear so often mentioned in Scriptural writing is the Syrian bear, distinctive for its gentle disposition.

The eagle seldom makes use of its beak in killing prey. Some animals are dispatched by the stroke of the eagle's dive, others are killed by the grip of its talons.

The otter sleeps in the water on its back.

There are four kinds of poisonous snakes in the United States—coral, copperhead, cottonmouth and several varieties of rattlesnakes.

Are You Dressed, Deer?

Hunters always are puzzled about how to figure how much his trophy deer weighed when it was on the hoof.

We weigh our deer only after all the fluids have been drained off and the innards are discarded. Gamemen say this amounts to 40 percent of its live weight.

Here are some typical weights at a glance:

DRESSED WEIGHT	LIVE WEIGHT (in pounds)
40	55
50	65
60	80
70	90
80	105
90	115
100	130
110	140
120	155
130	165
140	180
150	190
160	205
170	215
180	230
190	240
200	255

(They don't come much bigger)

Things You May Not Know

The milk snake is named for the erroneous belief that it milks cows. Though it frequents barns, it is attracted by mice, not cows.

The wings of the butterfly are colorful because they are

crossed by many minute ridges which break up the light into iridescent colors.

More than two hundred feathers make up the fan of the peacock.

Ladybugs do not die at the end of the season like so many other insects, but hibernate for the winter.

The legs of the penguin are enclosed in the skin of the body, thus making their walk slow and clumsy.

A bird's feet are so constructed that the foot is forcibly closed when the leg is bent. Hence birds maintain a steady grip on limbs or perches even when asleep.

The owls have an external ear, or conch, covered by feathers which exists in no other bird.

The parrot does not build a nest but lays its eggs in the soft dust that accumulates at the bottom of the trunks of decayed trees.

The eyes of hares are never closed. They have no eyelids, but are equipped with a thin membrane which covers the eyes when the animal is asleep or at rest.

The electric sparks from a cat's body when the fur is under friction are probably caused by the peculiar dryness of the hair which is free from the oily substances common to the coats of other animals.

The weasel is a very sound sleeper. It can often be taken up by the head, feet or tail and swung around for a considerable time before it awakens.

The butterfly fish often swims backward, its tail appearing to be its head.

The giant spider crab of Japan is the world's largest crab. It sometimes measures eleven feet from tip to tip.

There are more than seven thousand different kinds of ants.

The sassafras tree bears leaves in three different shapes.

The sting of a bee is located at the tail end of the abdomen.

A camel can drink twenty-five gallons of water in half an hour.

The pigeon is the only bird that drinks by suction. All other birds take the water into their mouths and throw their heads back in order to swallow.

The mockingbird can imitate at least thirty-two songs of other types of birds.

The giraffe is one of our strangest animals. He has no vocal cords, has fewer vertebrae in his neck than a mouse, is faster than a horse, can go longer without water than a camel, and can see backwards without turning his head.

The sloth, one of the slowest of all animals, eats so slowly that before he has finished one meal it is time for the next.

The dog wags his tail, but the hound wags his stern. An otter wags his pole, a rabbit his scut, a fox his brush, and a deer his single.

The skins of rats are used to make pocket books and tobacco pouches.

A primrose is not a rose. It is a perennial herb.

Hoe! Hoe! Hoe!

The best place a gardener can find a helping hand is at the end of his own sleeve.

The best time to weed your yard is right after your wife tells you to for the sixth time.

Why not plant weeds and see if the flowers will crowd them out?

Man's a funny creature: makes deserts bloom and lakes die.

The noise made by the ostrich is a roar, and at a distance it cannot be distinguished from that of a lion.

Plant more grass and flowers and you'll be satisfied with the life in your lot.

I knew a girl so dumb she thought cowslip was a bovine indiscretion.

When advised to use old cow manure on roses, the new gardener wondered how old the cow had to be.

In the spring, both gardeners and golfers begin plowing.

A beautiful garden is something most people will only turn over in their minds.

I know one lazy fellow who bragged about his phenomenal garden luck—nothing came up.

Usually a man who makes his own flower bed has to lie about it.

The gardener is the only man who can bring flowers to his wife for no reason at all and she won't get suspicious.

Plants weediest are seediest.

The best thing about vegetables is that there are no bones about it.

Lettuce may be a vegetable or a proposition—let us spray, let us prune, let us mulch, let us weed, let us!

Graffiti

Liberalism varies inversely with the age of the square.

The end of the world has been postponed for three weeks until the trumpeters learn their parts.

If you think a rabbit's foot is lucky, consider the original owner.

Remember when air was clean and sex was dirty?

The shortest distance between two points is always under construction.

The Population Bomb is everybody's baby.

Moby Dick Whales!

That is a four-letter word.

A Rolling Stone gathers groupies.

If God had wanted us to go to rock concerts He'd have given us tickets.

A bird in the hand makes it hard to blow your nose.

Repeal inhibition!

Grass is a root problem.

You don't have to be Jewish to wear Levi's.

Andy Warhol stencils!

God grades on the curve.

Old soldiers never die—young ones do.

Marijuana laws should be a joint legislative decision.

Beauty is only skin deep, but ugly is to the bone.

The world may be your oyster but it came out of polluted water.

X marks the spot for long lines at the movies.

Pessimists ought to have their dreads examined.

Heart donors are dead giveaways.

I shot an arrow into the air—and it stuck!

A gray rose is the symbol of pollution.

Poison ivy starts from scratch.

What gives you coffee nerves is the price.

The Lord giveth, but aphids, gophers, chinch bugs and cutworms taketh away.

The population explosion proves to heir is human.

A unicorn is a horny horse.

Hitchhikers are all thumbs:

You gotta have bread, man, before you can loaf.

Do wheat-growers have mi-grains?

Don't ditch throw-away bottles!

I have to take something every day for my kleptomania.

Before the Pill, babies were cheaper by the doesn't.

Old gardeners never die—they just spade away.

He who laughs—lasts!

Prejudice is being down on something you're not up on.

The population explosion keeps storkpiling.

Pollution costs prove grime does pay.

Perfect guests make the host feel at home.

Peat moss is loam on the range.

If you don't wear a smile you're not fully dressed.

Popullution is the problem.

Seat belts keep you hanging in there.

Life is a hereditary disease.

German hippies are flower Krauts.

Georgie-Porgie had bad breath.

The Galloping Gourmet has a pot hang-up.

Dow Jones is only average.

The most expensive fur-bearing animal is a mistress.

Jiminy Cricket bugs me!

A eunuch is a man cut-out to be a bachelor.

She who loves and loses has the wrong lawyer.

Pop corn, not pills.

Your future is shot-down if you shoot-up today.

Sissy firemen wear panty hose.

God is not dead! He is alive and autographing Bibles at Double-day.

Anyone who still thinks dirt is cheap hasn't priced topsoil lately.

Cattlemen know for whom the bull toils.

Power failure makes IBM a house of ill-compute.

How many shopping days until peace?

"Do dozens of jobs with one Jacobsen GT tractor."

Jerry Baker, America's Master Gardener

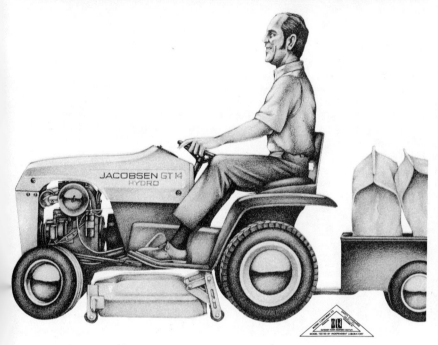

- Options include 42″ and big 50″ rotary mowers. Plus tiller, yard cart, lawn sweeper, dozer blade, snow thrower, many others.
- New Uni-frame design cradles and protects drive-train parts. And permits single in-line drive shaft to make best use of engine power without belts and pulleys.
- 12 and 14 HP hydrostatic drive models give you complete control of all forward and reverse speeds with one foot-pedal. No shifting. No clutching.
- 10 and 12 HP gear-drive GT tractor models also available.

JACOBSEN®

Jacobsen Manufacturing Company, Racine, Wisconsin 53403

A Member Company of Allegheny Ludlum Industries

how you spray

How you spray does make a difference. Only controlled, precise spray application—the kind you get with a Hudson sprayer—can give you *best* results in stopping insects, disease, and weeds. Here's why you'll find a difference—a *beautiful* difference—in your yard and garden when you use a Hudson sprayer . . .

right
reach & aim
One, you spray *right where the trouble is*—easily reach all parts of the plant—especially *under* the leaves where many bugs hide and most disease starts.

right
pattern
Two, *you* control the spray pattern—mist coarse, close up or long range, just wh needed.

which of these hudson sprayer

ladybug* garden protector
The fun way to spray! Looks like a friendly ladybug! Holds a gallon—enough for 40 rose bushes. Easy to use.

compression sprayers
Popular yard and garden sprayers because they do many and do them well. Ideal for spraying anything from the small trees. Offer more precise, controlled spray applica

hydra-gun® sprayer
Handy size—big performance. Sprays fine mist or long stream. Wonderful for flowers, small shrubs.

admiral* duster
Best way to apply dust. Long extension with adjustable nozzle makes it easy to dust under leaves. Powerful pump breaks up dust, assures uniform coverage.

hand sprayer
These handy s come in a type fo needs. Most mod smart, colorful "E lithography.

*Trademark   © MCMLXX II   H. D. HUDSON MA

Joes make a difference

or a beautiful garden...
better environment

Hudson Sprayers

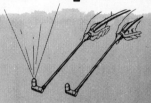

t

e, *you* mix the spray,
tly as recommended.
know the mixture
ht.

right amount

Four, with the control
valve *you* regulate the
amount you spray. Spray
just to the point of
run-off. No harmful
drenching, no waste.

right pressure

Five, you spray at the
pressure *you* select; high
pressure for a *fine mist*
(good for flowers), or low
pressure for a *wet spray*
(best for weeds).

d dusters meet your need?

ults. Easy to use—spray for an extended period without
ng. Available with 1½ to 4-gallon tanks of galvanized
ss steel. A model for every need or budget.

trombone® sprayer

For a long 30-ft. spray (ideal
for trees) or a fine close-up
mist, this is the sprayer.
Pumps easily—like a trom-
bone. Easy to carry.

suburban* power sprayers

Do big jobs quickly—easily. For all spraying—from
lawn to trees. 12½-gallon tank. Trail-N-Spray*
model (right) hitches to yard tractor.

porta* flame sprayer

New, versatile home tool.
Super-hot flame kills weeds,
melts ice, kills insects. Easy
to carry and use.

154 E. ERIE STREET • CHICAGO, ILLINOIS 60611

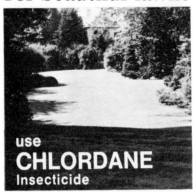